THE ULTIMATE SOCCER ALMANAC

BY DAN WOOG

Roxbury Park

LOWELL HOUSE JUVENILE

LOS ANGELES

CONTEMPORARY BOOKS

CHICAGO

Interior illustrations by Gary Torrisi
Photos provided by AllSport USA,
J. Brett Whitesell, and Corbis-Bettman
Roxbury Park is an imprint of Lowell House,
A Division of the RGA Publishing Group, Inc.

Publisher: Jack Artenstein
Editor in Chief, Roxbury Park Books: Michael Artenstein
Director of Publishing Services: Rena Copperman
Managing Editor: Lindsey Hay

Woog, Dan, 1953—
    The ultimate soccer almanac / Dan Woog.
       p.   cm.
    Includes index.
    Summary: Tells the history of soccer around the world as well as
in the United States, explains the laws of the game, and describes
the positions of the players.
    ISBN 1-56565-891-4
    1. Soccer—United States—History—Juvenile literature.
2. Soccer—History—Juvenile literature. [1. Soccer] I. Title.
GV944.U5W66   1998
796.334—DC21   97-42189
                                          CIP
                                          AC

Lowell House
2020 Avenue of the Stars, Suite 300
Los Angeles, CA 90067
Manufactured in the United States of America

10 9 8 7 6 5 4 3 2 1

THE ULTIMATE SOCCER ALMANAC

TABLE OF CONTENTS

INTRODUCTION

Many people think America's national pastime is baseball. After all, "Take Me Out to the Ballgame" is perhaps the only sports song *everyone* knows. Another American tradition is the Super Bowl. Each year on a Sunday in January, the entire country participates in a giant football festival. And of course, Michael Jordan and other NBA superstars can be seen everywhere, from the basketball courts to sneaker billboards to cereal boxes.

But a new tradition in the making is soccer. Within the last 20 years, when no one was looking, the game that *should* be called football (think about it!) sneaked up and surprised the whole nation. Today more boys and girls play organized soccer than just about any other sport. And every year the number of high school and college soccer teams grows.

In 1996 a professional league, Major League Soccer (MLS), roared into 10 cities across America. So many fans poured into the Los Angeles Galaxy's first home game that officials had to keep opening up sections of the 100,000-seat Rose Bowl to accommodate them.

The MLS's first championship match was another success. Torrential winds and rain pounded Foxboro Stadium in Massachusetts, but 40,000 spectators showed up to watch D.C. United storm from behind to win in sudden death overtime on a spectacular head goal. The players then celebrated wildly by sliding into a huge pile on the flooded grass.

That celebration is part of what makes soccer so special. It's not a game like basketball, where someone scores every few seconds. And it's not like football, baseball, hockey or any other team sport, where scoring is difficult but not rare.

Scoring in soccer is *tough*. The goal is big—eight feet high, eight yards wide—but just getting off a shot is hard. In soccer, when you have the ball, every opponent is a defender. The keeper covers the goal like a cat. And of course there is the added difficulty of trying to control the ball without your hands. Soccer players can use feet, heads, thighs, or chest—but no hands.

Yet the differences between soccer and other sports are also why soccer appeals to so many people. It combines many unique elements. Most of them do not require special physical features like enormous height or massive muscles. Think of a soccer player dribbling a ball through a crowd, cutting first one way, then the other before lacing a pass that a teammate controls with the flick of a foot. Or think of a defender leaping high in the air to clear a ball out of danger. These are things any sports fan can enjoy. They're as much a part of soccer as any goal. Of course, nothing compares to the sight of a player firing a long shot past a startled keeper, or extending her body full length to power a header into the far upper corner.

Millions of Americans, and billions of worldwide television viewers, saw those sights and many more during one glorious month in the summer of 1994. For the first time ever the World Cup—the most popular sports event on the planet—was played in the United States.

When the United States was announced as the host country seven years earlier, South Americans and Europeans laughed. Americans would never appreciate the ball skills of Brazilians or Argentines, they said, or understand the strategies used by Germans or Italians. Across the world, people predicted a World Cup disaster.

What they got was one of the greatest World Cups in history. For four exciting weeks, stadiums from Massachusetts to California were packed. Newspapers and television were filled with stories on players like Stoichkov, Baggio, Romario, and Maradona.

But Americans also watched, cheered, read, and heard about people named Harkes, Dooley, Wynalda, and Balboa—members of the U.S. national team. For the first time ever, the U.S. soccer team captured the imagination of the country. By finishing the first round of the World Cup with 1 win, 1 tie, and 1 loss, the U.S. team advanced to the round of 16 against the favorite—Brazil. The game was set for America's national holiday, July 4th.

More than 84,000 fans crammed Stanford Stadium in Palo Alto, California, to see if the United States could pull off the king of all upsets. America had not beaten Brazil in 64 years. In fact, in all that time we had not scored one goal against the Brazilian team!

Just 12 minutes into the game, U.S. player Thomas Dooley's shot seemed to be headed for the goal. Then, at the last second, it missed the net by inches. Near the end of the first half, Tab Ramos was injured, and the U.S. team's rhythm fell apart. Brazilian player Bebeto scored midway through the second half, and Brazil won 1-0. Brazil went on to win the entire World Cup, for a record fourth time, while the United States watched the rest of the tournament with everyone else, from the sidelines.

But the Americans had won something more important than the most popular trophy on earth. They had earned the respect of soccer fans everywhere. Even President Clinton invited them to the White House. The 1994 U.S. team showed that America was finally part of the soccer world. And they immediately started looking ahead to the 1998 World Cup in France.

Qualifying for France was not easy. As 1997 wound down, the U.S. team found itself in a precarious position. A few poor outings—including a 1-1 tie against Jamaica in Washington, D.C.—made the mood grim heading into an important match at Azteca Stadium in Mexico City, a place where the U.S. team had never won. The city's high altitude and heavy smog made running, even breathing, difficult.

But the Americans prepared well, spending three weeks high in the California mountains. They entered the early November match against Mexico with confidence. That attitude never wavered, not even when a defender was ejected for an overly aggressive foul, and they had to play a man down. By the end of the game, when it was clear the United States could escape with a tie, the crowd of 114,000 was on the Americans' side. They cheered every time the U.S. players touched the ball, and booed their own team lustily. The record books record it as a 0–0 tie, but it was truly one of the Americans' biggest victories.

The following Sunday, the U.S. team traveled north, to British Columbia, Canada, and shut out the Canadian team 3–0. That clinched a spot for the Americans at the 1998 World Cup, and cemented the emergence of the United States onto the world soccer stage.

It was an emergence that seemed sudden, but in reality it took years. Soccer in the United States dates back to the mid-19th century. Through the early and mid-20th century it was both an immigrant game and a prep school sport. But not until 1975, when Brazilian sensation Pele signed with the New York Cosmos of the North American Soccer League (NASL), was soccer seen as a true professional sport.

Pele's signing and the subsequent arrival of other superstars from around the globe spurred tremendous growth. Across America boys and girls began kicking soccer balls. They dragged their parents into the coaching ranks. As young players moved through youth leagues into the high school and college ranks, the standard of play rose dramatically. So did attendance at games and press coverage.

The NASL is no longer around (as much as it helped the current soccer boom, it was ahead of its time, and there were not enough fans to support the high-priced players imported from abroad), but Major League Soccer (MLS) is. Founded in 1996, MLS has pledged to avoid the mistakes of the past and build on the foundation of its predecessor.

As the U.S. national team prepared for the 1998 World Cup, it did so with a blend of players. There were veterans of previous tournaments, and newcomers who were just out of college. There were players based overseas, and those who competed in the MLS. There were players who came from suburban backgrounds, and those who grew up in urban areas. There were players who were Caucasian, African-American, and Hispanic. The U.S. national soccer team reflected the face of America.

This book will explore the world of soccer in all its many forms. From the original ball-and-goal games thousands of years ago, to the meetings in England where the first official rules were hammered out; from the famous teams of Europe and South America to the organization of the first World Cup in 1930. From the earliest stars to the latest superheroes of the U.S. women's national team, this book will cover it all. From the skills you need to play, to the rules you need to know, from soccer's many highlights to its lowlights, *The Ultimate Soccer Almanac* tells it all.

Part 1: Soccer Around the World

HISTORY OF SOCCER

The history of soccer extends far beyond the 1930 World Cup—the start of the game's modern era. The game stretches back to the 19th century—even longer, if you count 2,000-year-old writings from China about a ball-and-goal game similar to the one played today. The ancient Greeks and Romans also invented a version of soccer. However, most historians agree the game began 1,000 years ago in England, where entire villages played huge contests. Half the town would get on one side, attempting to kick a ball into the territory of the other half. Sometimes the balls were made of a pig's bladder; other times they used the skull of an enemy soldier. Things grew so

An 1875 engraving depicts the budding rivalry between England and Scotland.

violent that in 1314 King Edward II threatened to throw anyone playing the game into prison. Other kings tried the same thing, but their bans never held. People simply liked kicking a ball into a goal too much. It was fun; it felt good; it was nothing a king could stop.

The modern history of soccer dates back to the mid-1800s. People played ball-and-goal games throughout England. However, in every town the rules were different. Some places allowed carrying the ball; in others it could only be kicked. Some towns permitted pushing and tripping of opponents; others did not. Imagine how hard it was when teams from towns with different rules met.

The first attempt to create unified rules came in 1862. The next year brought the first meeting of the Football Association, an English group that still exists today. The result of these meetings was that two distinct games emerged. One did not allow holding the ball. We now call that game soccer. The other did allow holding the ball. It became known as rugby.

By the 1880s soccer players were getting paid. At the same time, the game started to spread around the world.

At the height of the British Empire, British sailors, soldiers, businessmen, teachers, doctors, and tourists traveled the seven seas in record numbers. Everywhere, the British influence was huge, and it extended to soccer. Men on every continent wanted to play this new, exciting game.

In 1863, a group of men called the Football Association hammered out special rules, and the game of soccer was born. The word "soccer" is a shortened version of "Association."

British sailors first played soccer in Brazil in 1874. A few years later, Charles Miller, a son of English immigrants, traveled from Brazil to England to study. He returned to South America with a few uniforms and soccer balls, and suddenly everyone there wanted to play too. The rest, as they say, is history.

British colonists introduced the game to Africa and Asia. It spread throughout Europe when Hungarians, Germans, Italians, Danes, and Dutchmen brought soccer back to their countries from England. By the beginning of the 20th century, there was hardly a spot on earth where soccer was not played.

In 1904 several countries met in Paris to form an international organization. They called it FIFA, which was French for Federation Internationale de Football Association. Surprisingly, the British stayed away from the meeting. They wanted to keep control of soccer for themselves. But by then soccer had become a world game, and they could not control it.

World War I slowed soccer's growth, but as soon as the war was over people began playing again. Now countries were competing against each other in stadiums instead of on battlefields. By the end of the 1920s, interest was high for a world championship.

THE WORLD CUP EXCITES THE GLOBE

Four European countries applied to host the first World Cup. However, FIFA awarded the tournament to Uruguay, because in 1930 that South American country would be celebrating 100 years of independence. Uruguay built a new stadium in the capital, Montevideo, and paid all travel and hotel expenses for the countries that came. However, because Uruguay was a three-week boat ride from Europe, only 13 teams applied. Among them was the United States. There was no qualifying tournament. Everyone was accepted.

The Americans looked strong, reaching the semifinals without giving up a goal. However, they were no match for Argentina, which beat the United States 6–1 to advance to the finals. But that was as far as Argentina got. Host Uruguay won the first World Cup, 4–2.

Four years later Uruguay became the only World Cup champion not to defend its title. Offended by most European countries' refusal to come to Uruguay in 1930, and upset by a players' strike, Uruguay chose not to travel to Italy for the second World Cup. But 32 countries did attend, and for the second time in a row the host country won. Italy defeated Czechoslovakia, 2–1.

World War II was about to break out in 1938, but the planet paused for the third World Cup just the same. France was the host. Italy celebrated two titles in a row, with a 4–2 victory over Hungary.

The war halted soccer's growth for 12 years. But by 1950 everyone was ready to return to sports. Brazil hosted the World Cup, which was won by neighboring Uruguay.

The 1950s saw soccer power shift to new countries. Two that suffered heavily in World War II, West Germany and Hungary, met in the 1950 World Cup finals in Switzerland. West Germany outlasted the Hungarians or "Magyars," 3–2.

An early U.S. team practices for the World Cup.

The 1958 World Cup, played in Sweden, was among the most famous in history. Brazil had already captured the imagination of the world with exciting superstars like Didi and Garrincha, but a 17-year-old sensation stole the headlines. His name was Pele (in Brazilian tradition, he went by one name only), and his dribbling and shooting skills were almost beyond description. The teenager led Brazil to a 5-2 thrashing of Sweden, and the game of soccer was never the same. The Brazilian style—creative moves and blinding speed—made "samba soccer" the rage.

Pele missed the 1962 World Cup in Chile—he was injured—but that did not stop Brazil. They won their second straight championship with a 3-1 victory over Czechoslovakia.

As exciting as that World Cup was, the next one four years later was even more so. For the first time ever, England—the birthplace of soccer—played host. In first round play North Korea, an unknown team, knocked off mighty Italy 1-0. In the quarterfinals Korea leaped out to a 3-0 lead over another good team, Portugal, but star Eusebio brought the Portuguese back to a thrilling 5-3 victory. The final between England and West Germany was tied 2-2 after 90 minutes. Suddenly, in overtime, Geoff Hurst slammed a shot off the underside of the goal post. To this day no one knows which side of the line the ball bounced down on. But the referee ruled it a goal, and his opinion is the only one that counts. Hurst added another goal a few minutes later, making him the first player ever to score three goals, or a "hat trick" in the World Cup finals.

Pele celebrating with teammate after winning the 1958 World Cup.

Brazil returned to center stage at the 1970 World Cup in Mexico. Pele led the way to his country's 4-1 victory over Italy. But a first-round game produced what many observers call the greatest save ever in soccer history. Pele timed his run and jump perfectly. His low header seemed sure to score. Yet suddenly England's goalkeeper, Gordon Banks, who thought the ball would go the other way, twisted incredibly in midair, and shoveled the wildly bouncing ball over the top of the net.

TOTAL SOCCER

At the 1974 World Cup, everyone was talking about "Total Soccer." That was the term given to the Dutch team led by Johan Cruyff, Johan Neeskens, and Johnny Rep. In "Total Soccer" players rotated positions constantly, moving up to attack and back to defend almost at will. With this system, the Netherlands scored the quickest goal in World Cup final history, on a penalty kick before West Germany even touched the ball. But the Germans fought back for the next 89 minutes, and stunned the Dutch 2-1.

The Netherlands was again the favorite in 1978, yet again the Dutch fell short. Argentina, the host, outlasted the "Total Soccer" team 3-1, although the rugged Argentine style was nowhere near as creative or pretty as the Dutch team's style.

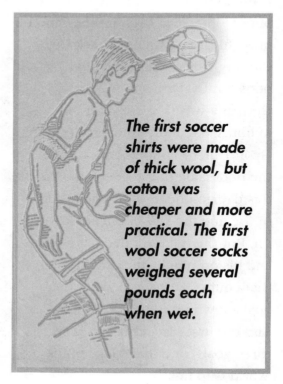

The first soccer shirts were made of thick wool, but cotton was cheaper and more practical. The first wool soccer socks weighed several pounds each when wet.

Italy won the 1982 finals in Spain, 3–1 over West Germany, but that World Cup will always be remembered for the amazingly dramatic semifinal game between West Germany and France. The teams tied 1–1 after regulation time. Both scored twice in overtime. France might have scored again on a penalty kick, but no call was made when German goalie Harald Schumacher brutally fouled Patrick Battiston. So the game went to penalty kicks. West Germany won that thriller, 5–4.

Mexico's 1986 World Cup was famous for Diego Maradona's "hand of God" goal. He used his hand to punch in a goal against England in Argentina's 2–1 quarterfinal win over England. The worldwide television audience saw the replay over and over. However, the referee did not, and the goal stood. West Germany made it to a record fifth World Cup final, but lost to Argentina 3–2.

The 1990 World Cup, held in Italy, was disappointing for a lack of goals, and because a number of stars turned in poor performances. Both semifinal games were decided on penalty kicks after the teams tied through overtime. The final also was decided on a penalty kick,

U. S. Team, 1994.

though this one came in regulation time. Andy Brehme's goal gave West Germany the title, 1–0 over Argentina.

In 1994, for the first time, the World Cup came to the United States. (The games at the Silverdome in Michigan marked the first time any World Cup game was played indoors.) The host Americans tied Switzerland 1–1, beat Colombia 2–1, then fell 1–0 to Romania. The U.S. team reached the second round, where it lost the July 4 thriller to Brazil, 1–0. The title game between Brazil and Italy produced the first scoreless final. In the penalty kick shootout to determine the winner, star Roberto Baggio blasted Italy's fifth kick over the bar—and Brazil was once again world champion.

FAMOUS TEAMS AROUND THE WORLD

With soccer now played in more than 200 countries, singling out the top teams of all time might seem impossible. But many of the same names pop up again and again. These are the teams that have left their mark on history. In fact, they're so famous that many American youth clubs have adopted their colors, even their names.

AJAX

This team from Amsterdam, in the Netherlands, has had a major impact on world soccer. It's also an old club, founded in 1900.

Ajax (pronounced "Eye-ax") has won all seven different club championships for which it is eligible. It is also one of only two teams to have won all three European championships (Italy's Juventus is the other).

Ajax's glory days began in the mid-1960s. The "Total Soccer" style that later

The first soccer shoes were ordinary work shoes. Players nailed studs into them to provide better traction.

became a Dutch trademark was born at Ajax. In "Total Soccer," players change position almost at will, moving up and down the field as attackers and defenders, replacing each other at a moment's notice. "Total Soccer" demands hard work, intelligence, and creativity. Fortunately, Ajax had the players to do it. They also had a coaching genius, Rinus Michels (pronounced "Ree-nus Mick-uls") who allowed his players complete independence.

Ajax's downfall began in 1973, when Johan Cruyff (Yo-hohn Krife)—the greatest player in Dutch history—was sold to Barcelona in Spain. But he returned a decade later as technical director, and under his guidance a new generation of players won the 1987 Winners' Cup. Though some of their top players have been sold to Italian clubs, Ajax continues to set the standard for Dutch soccer.

ARSENAL

This London club, named for the Woolwich Arsenal (a place where weapons and ammunition are stored), dates all the way back to 1886. Among its notable achievements are the introduction of the "stopper," and a history of championships beginning in the 1930s.

It took a long time after World War II for Arsenal to get back on top, but in the 1990s they did, winning several English and European championships.

Fittingly, Arsenal's nickname is the "Gunners."

BARCELONA

Barcelona may not be the biggest city in Spain—that honor goes to Madrid—but it boasts the best soccer team.

Barcelona has been helped twice by the presence of Dutch

The 1997 Barcelona team.

superstar Johan Cruyff. He arrived first as a player in the 1970s. He returned later as a coach. With players from across Europe—Ronald Koeman, Hristo Stoichkov, and Michael Laudrup, among others—Cruyff led them to the top.

When women's soccer first began in the Netherlands, men were not allowed to watch.

Barcelona won four straight league championships in the 1990s. Three were not decided until the final day. Even better for Barcelona fans, two of them came over Real Madrid, their biggest rival.

Barcelona's home stadium, Nou Camp, is one of the most famous in soccer. And with more than 100,000 dues-paying members, Barcelona is among the largest soccer clubs in the world.

BOCA JUNIORS

Along with River Plate, Boca Juniors is one of the most famous soccer teams in Argentina, and one of the most successful in the world. "Boca," as it is popularly known, was formed in 1905 by Europeans, including an Irishman named Patrick McCarthy, and several immigrants from Italy.

After several championships in the 1930s, Boca slipped a bit. But in the 1970s the team grew into one of the most powerful in South America. In 1981 Diego Maradona became the team's centerpiece. But a year later they needed cash, and sold him to Barcelona for $5 million.

CELTIC AND RANGERS

Mention Scottish soccer, and two names leap to mind: Celtic and Rangers. These two clubs, both based in Glasgow, are Scotland's best-known teams, and form one of international soccer's great rivalries.

Celtic, founded in 1888, achieved success first. In 1967 they were the first Scottish team to win the European Cup—along with the League, Cup, and League Cup championships. No team had ever done that before. However, financial problems led to Celtic's downfall, and in the 1980s Rangers took over the top spot in Scotland. Their success was inspired by player-coach Graeme Souness (pronounced "Graham Soo-niss"). Graeme did two things no one ever thought Rangers would do: He brought in English players (18 of them), and signed the first Catholic player, Mo Johnston. Prior to that, Rangers was entirely Protestant. Mo quickly proved himself to be a fan favorite, worth every penny of his $2.25 million contract.

FLUMINENSE

Though they have not won any international championships, Fluminense is known far beyond their home city of Rio de Janeiro, Brazil. Their stadium, Maracana (pronounced Mah-rah-kah-NAH), is the largest in the world. Over 170,000 spectators have crowded in for top matches, especially against crosstown rival Flamengo. Many of the Brazilian national team's home games are played at Maracana.

Some of the top players in soccer history have played for "Flu" (as the team is called), including Didi and Carlos Alberto. "Flu" fans honor their team by wearing white powder on their faces, a tradition that dates back to the turn of the century when the club was formed.

JUVENTUS

In the Italian language, Juventus means "youth," but this team from Turin has been around for more than a century. It was founded in 1897, and since then it has been a major supplier of players to the

Italian national team. For example, 1934 World Cup-winning goalkeeper Gianpiero Combi played for Juventus—and so did the goalkeeper and captain of the 1982 World Cup champions, Dino Zoff.

The 1997 Juventus team.

Juventus has signed stars from around the world. Among the players who wore the black-and-white striped shirts of the "Zebras" is French sensation Michel Platini. However, it is native superstars such as Paolo Rossi, Roberto Baggio, and Gianluca Vialli who have made Juventus the toast not only of Turin, but all of Italy.

DYNAMO KIEV

When nothing was going right in the former Soviet Union, people could always point with pride to Dynamo Kiev.

In 1975 Dynamo captured the Cup Winners' Cup, becoming the first Soviet team to win a European championship. Later that year they won their seventh Russian championship in 14 years.

The Soviet soccer federation thought that a club as strong as Dynamo could represent the entire nation at international matches. But the demanding schedule was too much for the team and they faded from the top. Ten years later, however, they once again won both the league and cup crowns.

When the Soviet Union collapsed in the early 1990s, Dynamo Kiev became the darling of a new country, Ukraine. Financial problems in Ukraine make the current soccer situation unstable, but no doubt Dynamo Kiev will be back in the international arena soon.

LIVERPOOL

Once upon a time, the name "Liverpool" meant "The Beatles." Earlier, it meant "soccer"; today, once again, it stands for the game, not the group.

Liverpool was founded in 1892. The club always did well, but it was not until the mid-1960s—around the time The Beatles put Liverpool on the world map—that the club achieved its greatest success. Kevin Keegan, Kenny Dalglish, and Graeme Souness are just three of the stars who brought championships to Liverpool. In 1986, with Kenny Dalglish as coach, Liverpool became one of the few English teams ever to win both the League and Cup championships.

Those titles were tarnished, however, by two stadium disasters during Liverpool games. In 1985, 39 people died and more than 400 were injured when English fans rioted, causing a wall to collapse an hour before the European Cup final against Juventus in Brussels, Belgium. Four years later, in Britain's worst sports disaster, 95 Liverpool fans were crushed to death and nearly 200 were hurt before an FA Cup semifinal in Sheffield. In that incident, crowds pushed forward at the start of the match, pinning others against security fences designed to keep them off the field.

MANCHESTER UNITED

Manchester United, one of the oldest and most popular clubs in the world, was founded in 1878.

The team (fondly known as "Man. U."), was the first English club to play in Europe in the mid-1950s. Soccer fans everywhere were thrilled when

Manchester United winning The Charity Shield in 1997.

Girls were not allowed to play soccer in English schools until 1991.

Man. U. reached the semifinals of the European Cup in 1958 with a hastily assembled team. Just a few months earlier they had lost eight players in an airplane crash in Munich.

It took a decade to recover, but in 1968 Manchester United was the European champion. Among the key players in that match, a 4–1 overtime win, were two crash survivors, forward Bobby Charlton (who scored twice) and defender Bill Foulkes. Coach Matt Busby had also survived the plane crash. A newcomer to the team was one of Northern Ireland's best and most flamboyant players, George Best.

Bryan Robson took over for Matt Busby as coach, and served until 1994. Along the way, Man. U. became only the fourth English team this century to win both the League and Cup championships. (The League championship is open to pro teams, while any club in the country—from the smallest to the biggest—can enter the Cup competition.)

AC MILAN

From the late 1980s through the present, AC Milan has been the most famous—and successful—soccer club in the world.

Silvio Berlusconi, a businessman who later became prime minister of Italy, invested $30 million in AC in 1986, turning it from bankruptcy to world club champion. Many people resented the owner's free-spending ways. He hired many international superstars, including Ruud Gullit, Marco Van Basten, Frank Rijkaard, and Franco Baresi, plus World Cup coach Arrigo Sacchi. But the team was exciting to watch, and they won trophies. And wherever they traveled around the globe, people paid to watch AC Milan play.

REAL MADRID

Before Barcelona, Real Madrid ruled Spanish soccer. Six times they were champions of Europe, 25 times of Spain. Both records still stand. In fact, they won so many titles

The 1997 Real Madrid squad.

that King Alfonso XIII added the title "Real"—meaning "Royal" (pronounced "Ray-ahl")—to the original club name "Madrid."

Real Madrid has been blessed with many legendary players, including Alfredo DiStefano of Argentina, Ferenc Puskas of Hungary, and Didi of Brazil. But perhaps the most famous man associated with the team was a former player who became coach and then president, Santiago Bernabeu. After the Spanish Civil War he organized a record-setting fund-raising drive to build a beautiful new stadium. The stadium (now named after Bernabeu) drew enormous crowds, which earned Real Madrid enough money to buy top players. That, in turn, helped them dominate soccer in the late 1950s and early '60s, the first years of the European Cup.

SANTOS

No soccer team in the world is associated so closely with one player as Santos is with Pele. Generally acknowledged as the greatest soccer player ever, the Brazilian superstar played virtually his entire career with this small club located not far from his home in São Paulo state.

Pele joined Santos in the mid-1950s, when he was just 15 years old. The spectacular, charismatic forward led his team to World Club Cup and South American Club Cup championships in 1962 and '63. But for years before and after, Santos toured the planet, constantly drawing sellout crowds.

The fans came to see Pele, but the money they paid enabled Santos to attract many other top players, including Gilmar and Zito. Unfortunately, all the travel and attention hurt many young players. They did not develop as slowly as they should have. By the end of the '60s Santos was no longer a team to be feared.

HISTORY'S GREATEST PLAYERS

FRANZ BECKENBAUER

It's not often that a player invents a new position, or stars with two different teams: one of the oldest in the world, and one of the newest. Or that after finishing a long and noted career he moves into coaching, and finds just as much success. But all those things, and much more, are part of the Franz Beckenbauer story.

The greatest German soccer player of all time—called "The Kaiser" in honor of his leadership abilities—has been a part of so many notable achievements it is hard to know where to begin. Perhaps the best place is with Bayern Munich. That is the club team where, with the encouragement of his coach, Beckenbauer invented the modern position of sweeper (also called "libero," meaning "free player"). Before Beckenbauer, defenders seldom ventured across mid-field. But he made things happen, because he was able to see everything happening in front of him, and reacted accordingly. The new position revolutionized soccer. All of a sudden, young players around the world *wanted* to be defenders.

In 1974 Beckenbauer was captain of the Bayern Munich team that won the European Cup. A few months later he captained an even more important team. He led the way as Germany captured the World Cup from the Netherlands.

Two years later, after setting a German record with 103 international appearances, "The Kaiser" stunned the world by transferring to the New York Cosmos of the NASL. Even though the Cosmos had signed Pele the year before, they were still largely a team of unknowns. Beckenbauer gave them a second star; suddenly the Cosmos were no longer just Pele and 10 other guys. With Beckenbauer directing the entire team from the back, the Cosmos won the NASL Soccer Bowl in 1977, '78, and '80.

Beckenbauer retired after the 1980 season, but in 1984 he was appointed German national team coach. The national team was not as strong as it had been when he was a player, but Beckenbauer the coach took them all the way to the 1986 final (they lost 3–2 to Argentina). The next time, in 1990, they went one better, winning the World Cup 1–0 over their old rival Argentina, in Rome. Never before had one man been both the captain and coach of two World Cup-winning teams.

In 1993, after a brief period coaching the French team Olympique Marseille, Beckenbauer returned to his original club, Bayern Munich, as executive vice president.

JOHAN CRUYFF

"Total Soccer" and "The Clockwork Orange," two terms from the 1970s, instantly bring Dutch soccer to mind. And when you talk about Dutch soccer, you have to start with Johan Cruyff.

In "Total Soccer" every player was able to play every position; they switched roles based on what was happening on the field, all game long. And no one did it better than Cruyff.

Wearing the orange jersey of the Netherlands, Cruyff started games at center forward. But he also pulled back into midfield and wandered to the wings. He was everywhere.

The "Orange Crush," one of the most exciting national teams ever, never won a World Cup. With Cruyff as captain they lost 2–1 in the 1974 finals to West Germany. But he had tasted success earlier. In 1972 he scored both goals at the European Cup final when his club team Ajax beat Internazionale of Italy. The next year his awesome 20-minute performance at mid-game led Ajax over another strong Italian team, Juventus.

Cruyff then left Ajax, the team he had joined at age 12 (his first-team debut came at 17). He moved to Barcelona in Spain, and won three European Football of the Year Awards there.

In 1978 Cruyff followed Pele and Franz Beckenbauer to the United States. He joined the Los Angeles Aztecs of the NASL, and was soon named Most Valuable Player. He later played with the Washington Diplomats. He returned to the Netherlands, and as coach with his old club Ajax won the European Cup Winners' Cup in 1987 and '89. Five years later he did the same thing with his other old club, Barcelona.

Today Cruyff's son is also a professional player—hoping to follow in his father's footsteps.

EUSEBIO

While Pele was known as the "Black Pearl," Eusebio was called the "Black Panther." Those nicknames described their differences. Pele was cool and smooth, Eusebio (pronounced You-SAY-bee-oh) was quick and strong.

Eusebio grew up in Mozambique, a Portuguese colony in Africa, and was the first African soccer superstar. His arrival in Portugal in 1961 was interesting. The Sporting Lisbon team heard about him and brought him in for a tryout. But officials from Sporting's main rival, Benfica, "kidnapped" him off the airplane, and signed him.

In 13 seasons Eusebio brought Benfica to the top of international soccer. He was European Football Player of the Year in 1965, and top scorer (nine goals) in the 1996 World Cup, when Portugal finished third. His rivalry with Pele was intense. (Interestingly, they both spoke Portuguese, because that is also the native language of Brazil.) Several times, when their club or national teams met, he outplayed "the greatest player of the world."

Eusebio ended his career in the NASL, with the Boston Minutemen, Toronto Metros-Croatia, and Las Vegas Quicksilver. But he continued to be loved in Portugal, for his strong play as well as his great sportsmanship. Today a statue of Eusebio stands at the entrance to Benfica's stadium.

DIEGO MARADONA

Though clearly one of the greatest players in history, Diego Maradona is also one of the most controversial. Many problems, including his rough style of play, unsportsmanlike attitude, and drug problems, have made him a poor role model for young soccer fans the world over.

Maradona led Argentina to the heights of international soccer. In 1986 the South American nation won the World Cup finals, 3-1 over West Germany.

Maradona was captain of the Argentine team, and unanimous choice as Player of the Tournament. However, he is still best remembered for his "Hand of God" goal against England in the quarterfinals, when he punched the ball past the keeper with his hand. The only person in the stadium at Mexico City who did not see that illegal act was the referee. Maradona's other goal in that match, a spectacular solo effort in which he beat five defenders and goalkeeper Peter Shilton during a 60-yard run, was almost forgotten in the controversy.

Maradona also scored another great goal in that tournament, against Belgium in the semifinals. Then, in the finals, his brilliant pass to Jorge Burruchaga proved to be the game-winner.

In 1990, though injured, Maradona again helped Argentina to the finals. This time, however, they lost, 1-0 to West Germany.

But the next spring, while he was playing with Napoli in Italy, a drug test showed that Maradona had been using cocaine. He was suspended from soccer for 15 months. When he returned to Argentina, Maradona was arrested for cocaine possession. He tried several comebacks, but continued to have problems with both drugs and weight. In 1994, he was banned from the World Cup after again failing a drug test.

Those were just the latest of Maradona's many problems. As far back as 1982 he was in trouble. During that World Cup, in Spain, he was red-carded for a brutal tackle on a Brazilian player. Maradona's reputation—both for poor sportsmanship and drug use—will remain with him forever.

SIR STANLEY MATTHEWS

What's a soccer player doing with "Sir" in front of his name?

In the case of Sir Stanley Matthews, it's because the Queen of England made him a knight.

Matthews, as he was known then, was the first great English player after World War II. Because England had suffered so much for so many years during that war, his great play, and the honor it brought his country, was important to every Englishman, whether they were soccer fans or not. Accordingly, the Queen knighted him.

Matthews's fame came as a dribbler. He played right wing in the days when teams used five forwards. And he had so many fakes and moves, not even the greatest defender could stay with him.

But Matthews did not win a championship until he was 38. Playing in the FA (English League) Cup final, his team, Blackpool, was losing 3-1 to Bolton. Very little time remained. But then Matthews went to work, dribbling this way and that through the Bolton defense. Blackpool scored twice in the last three minutes. In overtime, Matthews provided the assist on the winning goal.

Thirty-eight is old to play professional soccer—but Matthews continued to play for a remarkable 12 more years, until he was 50. And he not only played, but he starred. He helped his final team, Stoke City, advance from the Second to the First Division. When he retired in 1965, after an incredible 33-year career, his farewell game attracted the top players in the world. Most had not even been born when Matthews— Sir Stanley—first started dribbling.

PELE

Entire books could be written about Pele, the small man with the short name and the greatest soccer skills in the world. Pele's accomplishments could fill volumes. Simply put, he is the best player ever, and also one of the most respected.

Pele grew up poor in a small town near São Paulo, Brazil. But by the time he was 15, the Santos club bought his contract from his local team, Bauru. The next year Pele made the national team; by 17 he was playing in the 1958 World Cup in Sweden. He became the youngest player ever to win soccer's top prize.

And not just win, but star. Pele—whose real name is Edson Arantes do Nascimento; he cannot remember how he got his nickname—

scored two goals in the final, helping Brazil to a 5–2 victory over host Sweden.

Four years later Brazil tried to repeat as world champions. Pele scored a beautiful goal against Mexico in the first round, but then pulled a muscle and missed the rest of the World Cup. However, Brazil again won the title.

The rest of 1962 and '63 went better for Pele. Santos won the World Club championship both years. Constant world tours exposed Pele to an international audience. They thrilled to his magical dribbling ability. The ball seldom seemed to leave his foot, even in a crowd thick with defenders. They loved his feints and fakes, and admired his booming shots. In his career, Pele scored more than 1,000 goals.

But as much as they liked Pele the player, soccer fans around the globe loved Pele the man. He had time to talk to spectators; he was never sad; and no one could resist his million-watt smile.

When Brazil tried to win a record third world championship in 1970, everyone rooted for Pele. He did it—he led his country to yet another World Cup crown. He retired in 1973.

But Pele loved soccer too much to stay away forever. In 1975 the New York Cosmos, a struggling team in the struggling NASL, signed him for $4.5 million. It was the most incredible sports story of the year. Suddenly, people across America were interested in soccer; the greatest player ever was coming to New York. For three years, wherever the Cosmos played, enormous crowds followed. Before and after the NASL season, the Cosmos toured the world. Almost single-handedly, Pele brought soccer to the American masses, and brought the Cosmos to the globe.

In 1977, after leading the Cosmos to the Soccer Bowl championship, he retired again. His farewell match was held at brand-new Giants Stadium. A crowd of 77,000 turned out to bid farewell to "The King." He played half the game with the Cosmos, half with his old team Santos. When he took his final lap around the field, 77,000 soccer fans had tears in their eyes.

In 1984 FIFA, the world governing body of soccer, presented Pele with its Gold Medal Award for outstanding service to the game. Today, back home in Brazil, Pele serves his government as minister of sport.

LEV YASHIN

It's not easy to pick the greatest goalkeeper ever, but a good case could be made for Lev Yashin (pronounced Yah-sheen).

During the 1950s and early '60s, when much of the world looked down on the Soviet Union for its harsh communist rule, Yashin made friends for his native land. He was an iron man in the goal, leading Russia to the gold medal at the 1956 Olympics, and reaching the quarterfinals of the 1958 World Cup. He also helped his team capture the first European championship in 1960. Yashin played in two other World Cups, and throughout his career he saved more than 150 penalty kicks.

Yashin was a tremendous keeper, with long arms and quick reflexes, but he also was a great sportsman. In 1963 he was the first Russian player to be named European Footballer of the Year, and remains the only goalkeeper ever to win the award. When a South American magazine polled readers to pick the Greatest Team of All Time, Yashin was the runaway goalkeeper winner. His 1970 farewell retirement match in Moscow drew 100,000 fans, and top players from all over the world.

In some Middle Eastern countries, men are prohibited from attending women's soccer matches. It is against religious law for a man to see a woman's legs in public.

FAMOUS PLAYERS TODAY

ROBERTO BAGGIO
Midfielder

The Italian-born Roberto Baggio turned professional in 1982, at the young age of 15. Within three years he was playing with the famous club Fiorentina. After the 1990 World Cup, hosted by his native country, Roberto was sold to Juventus of Turin for $20 million. In 1993 he led Juventus to the UEFA Cup championship, and was

Baggio (number 10) sizing up the ball.

named both FIFA World Player of the Year and European Player of the Year. In 1995 he signed a contract with AC Milan, one of Juventus's main rivals. He and his new teammate, George Weah, helped Milan to the 1996 European Cup Winners' Cup title.

But for all those accomplishments, Roberto Baggio will probably always be remembered for a goal he did not score. In the finals of the 1994 World Cup, at the Rose Bowl in California, he missed the final penalty kick that allowed Brazil to win. He was not the only player to miss that day, but because he was the most famous, he became the goat.

Of course, without Roberto the Italians might never have made it to the finals. He scored several great goals, though none was as exciting as the one four years earlier against Czechoslovakia. That was named the best goal of the 1990 World Cup.

In 1997 Roberto Baggio transferred to Bologna, another club in the Italian *Serie A*.

Best strength: Roberto Baggio likes to slash forward on the attack.

ERIC CANTONA
Striker

Eric (right) mixing it up during time out.

Though he is a Frenchman, Eric Cantona is perhaps the most famous player in English soccer since Sir Stanley Matthews and Gordon Banks more than 30 years ago.

Eric, who was born in Paris in 1966, has always been a moody, off-and-on player. But no one has ever doubted his skill. Ever since he arrived in England in 1992 he has been a winner. He led Leeds United and Manchester United to English League championships, the only time a player won back-to-back titles with different clubs. In fact, he won a championship every season he competed in England. (Earlier, he won French titles with Marseille and Montpellier.)

In 1994 the English soccer association honored him by naming him the first foreigner to win the Footballer of the Year trophy.

But Cantona's reputation suffered in 1995, when he attacked a Crystal Palace fan. He was convicted of assault, and banned from soccer for nine months. Two years earlier he had been suspended for four games, following a wicked foul in a Champions League match.

Before that, when the French soccer league banned him after a series of red cards he left the country, and called French soccer officials "idiots." He retired from soccer in spring 1997.

Best strength: Eric Cantona's unpredictability with the ball makes him difficult to defend.

RYAN GIGGS
Midfielder/Striker

Ryan Giggs, a young Welshman, is perhaps the most famous player in the English League today. He's been a fixture at Manchester United since the age of 17 when he scored the only goal in his very first match, a 1–0 victory over hated rival Manchester City in 1991.

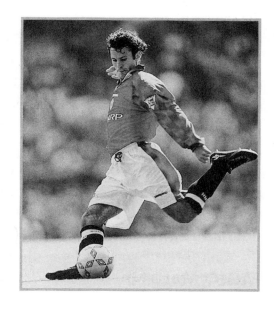

Ryan, who plays both center forward and central midfield, has a history of firsts. He was the youngest player ever on the Welsh national team (17 years, 321 days), and the first player ever to win the English Soccer Association's Young Player of the Year award two years in a row (1992 and '93).

Ryan is not a great goal scorer. He makes his mark by beating defenders with a burst of speed, then lacing crosses for teammates to run on to. His performance dipped a bit in the mid-1990s, but he returned to form in 1995, and beyond.

Thanks in great part to Ryan, in 1996 Manchester United won both the Premier and Champions League titles.

Best strength: Ryan Giggs beats defenders with blistering speed, then lofts dangerous crosses into the goal mouth.

STEVE McMANAMAN
Midfielder

Most English soccer fans love one team, and hate all the rest—especially crosstown rivals. But Steve McManaman is a soccer player as well as a fan, and even though he grew up cheering for Everton, he realized that hated Liverpool was better suited to his patient, passing style of play.

He signed with Liverpool on his 18th birthday in 1991, and 10 days later made his debut with the first team. He scored in his second start and played 32 league games that season, more than any other forward.

McManaman joined England's national team in 1994, and continued to star for Liverpool. He shifted to right midfield, continued to score great goals, and looks as if he will be an English star for years to come.

Best strength: Steve McManaman has great dribbling skills.

PAOLO MALDINI
Defender

Paolo Maldini knows soccer. Not only does he captain the Italian national team, but his father, Cesare, is the coach. A few years ago Cesare Maldini coached Paolo on the national Under-23 team. That team won the European youth championship three times.

Paolo reached the top Italian division, *Serie A*, at the age of 16 with AC Milan. By

1996 he was accomplished enough to place second to George Weah in voting for FIFA World Football Player of the Year. *World Soccer* magazine named him World Player of the Year two years before that, the first defender ever to win the award.

Maldini is a left fullback, yet often goes up on the attack. In fact, he is considered the best attacking fullback in soccer today. He tackles hard, then moves forward just as intently and lofts dangerous crosses into the box.

His contract with Milan runs through the year 2000, but he is liable to stay with them much longer. Milan is his hometown, and it is the club his father captained in 1963.

Best strength: Paolo Maldini wins tackles, then goes forward hard on offense.

ALESSANDRO DEL PIERO
Midfielder

The next superstar in Italian soccer could well be Alessandro del Piero.

"Ale," as del Piero is called by his teammates, is not particularly tall, but his great ball control and sharp passing ability make him a superb midfielder. At Juventus of Turin, he has become known for his perfect shots from the left into the upper right hand corner of the net. The area has been called the "Del Piero Zone."

In 1994, just 18 years old, Alessandro helped Juventus win the Italian League Cup championship, and reach the finals of the European Cup. When teammate Roberto Baggio held out for more money, the Juventus management decided that because they had Alessandro, the former World Cup star was expendable. He now wears Baggio's former number 10, and his coach and fans call him "untouchable."

Best strength: Alessandro Del Piero has a deadly left foot.

ROMARIO
Striker

When Brazil won the 1994 World Cup, they had Romario to thank. He was awarded the Golden Ball as the tournament's best player, and also earned the Bronze Shoe as the third highest scorer (five goals).

Romario, who was born in 1966 in Rio de Janeiro, first drew world attention during the 1988 Olympics, when Brazil lost in the final to the Soviet Union. He was signed by PSV Eindhoven, and stayed with that Dutch team for five years. After scoring 98 goals for PSV he moved on to Barcelona. Although he was the top scorer in Spain, he did not get along with his coach, Johan Cruyff. The year after winning the World Cup he quit to return to Brazil, where he played for Flamengo.

In 1997 Romario led the Brazilian national team to victory at Copa America (the South American championship) in Bolivia. He returned to European soccer that same year, playing for Valencia in Spain. He continues to be deadly in the penalty area, scoring important goals game after game.

Best strength: Romario is quick and agile in the penalty area.

RONALDO
Striker

He was FIFA's World Player of the Year in 1996, at the tender age of 20. Called his country's greatest player since Pele, Ronaldo— instantly recognizable by his shaved head—led Brazil to its first Copa America (South American) championship in 1997, scoring five goals.

Ronaldo was born in the slums of Rio de Janeiro. At 13 he traveled for two hours on two buses to try out for his favorite team, Flamengo. He made the first cut, but had no money to return the next day.

But Ronaldo was spotted at age 14 by Jairzinho, another Brazilian star, and within two years was playing in the Brazil First Division. He scored 54 goals in 54 games for Cruzeiro Belo Horizonte, a goal-a-game feat not even Pele managed when he was that young.

All the top clubs in the world wanted Ronaldo, but in 1994 he signed with PSV Eindhoven in the Netherlands. He ended his first season as the nation's top scorer, with 35 goals, and his team won the Dutch Cup.

After another season with Eindhoven, Ronaldo moved to Barcelona, where he scored one of the most exciting goals in Spanish history. He received a pass near midfield, sped past five defenders— half the opposition—and finished with a walloping 40-yard shot. The replays were still being shown many months later.

After a year with Barcelona, his contract was purchased by Italy's Inter Milan, for a whopping $56 million. A crowd of 55,000 turned out for his first game—and it was only an exhibition match.

Ronaldo's soccer talents include spectacular moves, quick reflexes, great physical strength, explosive speed over short and medium distances, and a tremendous hunger for the ball. But he is also an excellent role model for young players. Ronaldo is well-behaved, patient with fans and the media, drinks nothing stronger than mineral water, and often thanks his mother for letting him play soccer when he was young.

Best strength: Ronaldo has an amazing ability to hold the ball while dribbling through swarms of defenders.

PETER SCHMEICHEL
Goalkeeper

Goalkeepers keep getting bigger and better. But it's hard to imagine anyone bigger—or better—than six-foot, four-inch star Peter Schmeichel.

Peter burst on the world scene in 1992, when little-heralded Denmark won the European championship. Danish players were not as well known as English, Spanish, French, and Italian players, but Peter proved it's not where you come from, but how you play that counts.

The European championship showcased Peter to the rest of the world, and he left the Danish league for Manchester United in England. In 1993 he set a team record by playing in more than 90 straight games. At one point in 1996, he went 1,135 minutes—more than 12 consecutive games!—without giving up a goal.

But Peter was not always a star goalkeeper. He started his career as a striker, with the Gladsaxe team in his Danish hometown. Many years later, in 1996, he showed he still could score. His Manchester United coach sent him forward on a corner kick, and he scored on a header. The year before, he helped the team achieve the rare "double," winning both the league and cup championships.

Peter relaxes with music. He plays piano, drums, flute, and guitar (his father is a professional pianist). "I'm so involved in soccer, I find music relaxing," he says. "When I get home I want to throw the boots away and enjoy something else."

Best strength: Peter Schmeichel controls the entire penalty box, and is an absolute perfectionist.

ALAN SHEARER
Striker

When Alan Shearer was the top scorer at the 1996 European Championship, his performance paid instant dividends. The club team Newcastle United paid Blackburn Rovers what was then a record amount (£15 million) to sign him to a contract.

For Alan, a center forward and the best goal scorer in English soccer, that transfer meant a chance to go home. He was born in Newcastle in 1970. However, his home team rejected him when he was young, only 14, and he had to go clear across England, to Southampton, to get his first contract.

Alan is so calm on the field, some people call him boring. But his touch on the ball is so clean, his running so steady, and his "nose for the goal" so sure, it does not matter how unflashy he is. He scores goals, and that's why Newcastle wanted him so badly.

Alan has played on the English national team since 1994. In 1995 he was named English Player of the Year.

Best strength: Alan Shearer's first touch is superb, and he never gets rattled.

CARLOS VALDERRAMA
Midfielder

Some athletes are recognized for their skill, others for their style. Carlos Valderrama—"El Pibe," or "The Kid"—is known for both.

As captain of Colombia's national team—a frequent World Cup participant—for nearly a dozen years he has represented his country more than 100 times in international competition. He has played in five Copa America (South American championship) tournaments since 1987. Twice he was voted South American Player of the Year.

Yet even if you did not notice Carlos's creative midfield talents, you would not be able to miss him. His enormous head of red dreadlocks makes him one of the most recognizable players in the world. That recognition helped the new United States pro league, MLS, when he joined the Tampa Bay Mutiny in 1996 in its very first season. He was named Most Valuable Player that first year for his hard, exciting work. His daring dribbling and precision passing earned him fans wherever the Mutiny played.

Before MLS, Carlos played with Montpellier in France and Real Valladolid in Spain. He then moved back to Colombia to play for two

more teams, Deportiva Independiente Medellin and Atletico Junior.
Best strength: Carlos Valderrama is a creative passer and precise dribbler.

GEORGE WEAH
Striker

In 1995 George Weah became the only man ever to be named FIFA World Player of the Year, European Footballer of the Year, and African Football Player of the Year the same year. He was also the first African ever to win the FIFA and European titles.

Weah's career began in his native Liberia, where he was born in 1966. George soon moved to Cameroon. In 1988 he joined Monaco in the French League, where he stayed for four seasons. In 1992 he transferred to Paris Saint-Germain, winning the prestigious "African Golden Ball" trophy in 1989 and 1994. He was noted for his acrobatic play and swift attacking skills.

After winning several championships, including two French Cups, George decided to test himself in the toughest league in the world: the Italian *Serie A*. He transferred to AC Milan, and in 1996 his new team won the European Cup Winners' Cup.

But George has never forgotten his native country. He set up the George Weah Foundation, which provides funds to people affected by Liberia's civil war, he organized several fund-raising exhibition games for the Liberian national team around the world, and gives money to help Liberia's World Cup effort.

George, who is married to an American woman, hopes one day to play for an MLS team. He has friends and family in New York City, and owns several houses and a restaurant there. After he retires, George plans to work for UNICEF (United Nations Children's Fund), and the causes of international peace and hunger relief.

Best strength: George Weah bursts through opponents with power and speed.

IAN WRIGHT
Striker

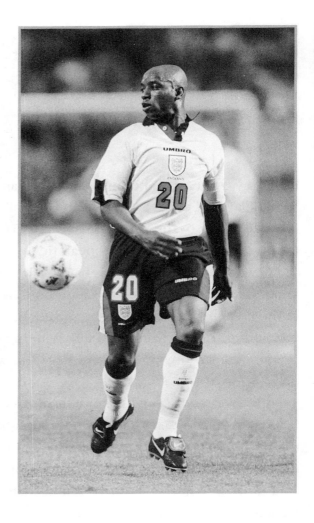

What's a little thing like a broken leg, when you've got a chance to play in the English FA Cup final?

Not much, to Ian Wright. Despite having broken his leg twice, the Crystal Palace striker came off the bench in 1990 to score twice, helping his team to a 3-3 tie with Manchester United. It was not enough—Palace lost the rematch—but it showed what Ian was made of.

The following season he scored 15 goals, and Crystal Palace finished third in the league. That convinced Arsenal to pay a record amount for his contract, and in his very first league game of the next season their investment proved good. Ian scored a hat trick against Southampton, and Arsenal was on its way.

When he was 33 years old he retired from international competition, but he is still one of the most feared strikers in England. He remains a fan favorite, too.

Best strength: Ian Wright is a consistent goal scorer.

TONY YEBOAH
Striker

The English team Leeds bought Tony Yeboah's contract in 1995 on a gamble. The coach had never seen the striker from Ghana play, but still they paid a record amount for him.

The gamble paid off. Tony's near goal-a-game scoring pace made Leeds a contender. And the goals he scored were so great, fans flocked to see him. When the season began, he won the English League Goal of the Month Award not once, but twice in a row.

Leeds was willing to gamble on Tony because of what he had done with the Einracht Frankfurt club. He was the Bundesliga (German League) leading scorer for two years, with 38 goals in 48 games.

But in 1997 Leeds had a new coach, and Tony did not get along with him. So he made an incredible offer to any team anywhere in the world. He guaranteed that he *would* score 15 goals the following season. If he did not, he would return half his salary.

"I'm one of the 10 best strikers in the world," he said, explaining his confidence that he would reach the magic 15 mark.

Best strength: Tony Yeboah scores spectacular goals.

Part II: Soccer in America

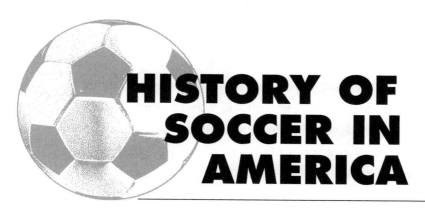

HISTORY OF SOCCER IN AMERICA

IN THE BEGINNING

American soccer has been called a "hybrid." That means it's a combination of things. The American style of play combines the teamwork and solid defense of the Europeans with the flair and creativity of South Americans. That's logical; after all, the United States itself is a mixed bag of cultures. Americans come from all over the globe, so it makes sense that our soccer history is tied up with many different cultures.

Soccer started here even before the Pilgrims landed at Plymouth Rock. Native Americans were playing ball-and-goal games centuries ago. But as we have seen, it was the English who really popularized the game in the mid-1800s, and they brought it to their former colony, the United States, just as they did to the rest of the world.

The first organized club in the United States, the Oneidas, was undefeated from 1862 to 1865. A few years later, Princeton and Rutgers played what is called the first college football game ever, but it was actually more like a combination of soccer and rugby than what Americans now call "football."

Over the next several decades, soccer and football developed into completely different games. As football boomed on college campuses, soccer was being played by European immigrants nationwide. It was fun, inexpensive weekend entertainment for men who worked hard all week in factories and mills.

By the 1920s, excellent leagues had formed in many parts of the country. There were teams of Scots, Englishmen, Poles, Italians, and

Germans. There was even the American Professional Soccer League (APSL), though no one made enough money at the game to quit his full-time job as a bricklayer, welder, or factory worker. In fact, the APSL continued, in various forms, all the way through 1984.

But for many years soccer remained a minor sport in America. Still, America had its moments of soccer glory. In 1920 the United States was one of 13 countries to compete in the first World Cup, in Uruguay. The American players (six of whom were ex-English professionals) were big and bulky—not typical builds for soccer players—but they showed they could play the game by beating Belgium and Paraguay by identical 3-0 scores. Then, in the semifinals, they ran into the Argentina buzzsaw, and lost 6-1.

In 1941 10 men formed the National Soccer Coaches Association of America. Today the organization has more than 10,000 members, but back then it was just a dot on the high school and college sports landscapes. The big sports were football, basketball, and baseball. Hardly anyone cared about soccer. It was still seen as a game played by immigrants in cities. That image continued throughout the 1950s.

That is why hardly anyone noticed what happened on June 29, 1950, in faraway Belo Horizonte, Brazil. The first World Cup in

History books say the first college football game in America was played in 1869 between Princeton and Rutgers, but the game was actually soccer. The confusion comes because back then, soccer was also called "football."

12 years was being held (World War II caused the cancelation of the 1942 and 1946 games), and the United States was playing England, one of the strongest teams on earth.

The American players hardly knew each other. There were a few players from St. Louis, several from the East Coast, a Scotsman, and Joe Gaetjens from Haiti. The goalie, Frank Borghi, worked full-time as an undertaker. They didn't seem to stand a chance. The only question was by how many goals would they lose.

But Borghi made a few key saves, and a few English shots hit the post. Then, near the end of the first half, something truly unexpected happened: Gaetjens scored on a header. No one knows if he really tried to shoot or the ball took a lucky bounce off his head, but today that does not matter. The Americans had scored, and for the next hour they hung on for dear life.

The 1–0 final score was so amazing, no one could believe it. A newspaper editor in England was certain someone had made a mistake, and changed the score to read England 10, America 1.

That was the high point of American soccer, between 1930 and 1975, and it did not last very long. The United States went on to lose its very next World Cup game, 5–2 to Chile, and came home. There were no parades, no newspaper articles, certainly no television coverage. Joe Gaetjens went back to working for the post office. A few years later he returned to Haiti, and was never heard from again.

College soccer began to grow a few years later, and in 1959 the first college championship was held. St. Louis University won the title that year, and the next. They were one of the few college teams with only American-born players.

THE BIRTH OF THE NASL

In 1960 a new pro league was formed. The International Soccer League imported entire teams from Europe and South America. Crowds occasionally exceeded 20,000, though most were smaller. But that piqued the interest of businessmen in this "new" game, and by 1967 they formed what they called a "major soccer league": the North American Soccer League (NASL).

From 1967 to 1974 the NASL grew slowly. Crowds were small, newspaper and television coverage was tiny, but at least American fans were seeing good soccer. In 1973 Kyle Rote Jr., whose father had been a famous football player, became the first American and first rookie to capture the league scoring title. The next year he won ABC-TV's "Superstars" competition against athletes from sports like football, basketball, and baseball, causing many people to wonder what made soccer athletes so superior. But still the NASL was a minor league, and soccer remained a minor sport.

THE COMING OF PELE

All that changed the summer of 1975. The New York Cosmos were a team with players named Siggy Stritzl, Mordecai Shpigler, and Joey Fink. They played at Randalls Island, a dilapidated stadium underneath a bridge. Hardly anyone, even in New York, had ever heard of the Cosmos.

Suddenly, the whole world knew who they were. That June they signed Pele, the greatest soccer player ever. He had retired a few years earlier, but was still only 34 years old. He could dribble, pass, and shoot with the best of them; he had a smile that could light up an entire stadium, and the entire planet recognized his name. Even people who had never heard of the Cosmos or the NASL knew and loved Pele. (President Gerald Ford even asked him to visit the White House!)

Pele's first Cosmos game, against the Dallas Tornado, drew a capacity crowd of 21,000 fans, seven times the Cosmos's average—and a national television audience. Pele scored the tying goal on an amazing header, and a new era in American soccer had begun.

Throughout that 1975 season, crowds continued to grow. The Cosmos did not win the NASL championship—even Pele could not produce a miracle—but they were suddenly the most famous team on earth. They started touring in the off-season, traveling as far as China. Now, all the world knew about American soccer.

The next year the Cosmos moved to Yankee Stadium and added another superstar, Italian striker Giorgio Chinaglia. Other NASL teams rushed to add big names. Portuguese star Eusebio came to the Boston Minutemen; the San Antonio Thunder signed English World Cup hero Bobby Moore; fellow Englishmen Rodney Marsh and George Best went to the Tampa Bay Rowdies and Los Angeles Aztecs, respectively. Every big-name soccer player, it seemed, wanted to come to America.

Crowds swelled to 50,000, 60,000, and beyond. The Cosmos did not win the Soccer Bowl championship that year either (the Toronto Blizzard did), but 1977 promised to be different.

For the second straight season, the Cosmos changed homes. Brand-new Giants Stadium became the "in" place to be. Crowds as large as 77,000 came to watch Pele and the Cosmos's newest superstar, Franz Beckenbauer, captain of World Cup champion West Germany. The Cosmos also featured players from Ireland, England, Peru, even South Africa. Everyone knew this was to be Pele's last year, and his teammates finally came through with a championship. In the Soccer Bowl championship, the Cosmos beat the Seattle Sounders 2–1.

Six weeks later, another sellout crowd turned out for Pele's farewell game, an exhibition

The first shin guards were leather, with wool lining. They were worn over the socks.

against his old club team, Santos of Brazil. He took the microphone, told everyone to "Love! Love! Love!" each other and soccer, and then it was over. After three exciting years, American soccer once again had to move on.

Could the NASL survive Pele's retirement? For a few years, it did. Stars like Johan Cruyff continued to come to America. But the league had expanded too fast—at one point there were 24 teams—and there was too much of a gap between the big clubs like the Cosmos and Los Angeles Aztecs, and the smaller ones like the Tulsa Roughnecks and Jacksonville Teamen. There were high salaries, but no television contract. In 1985 the league folded. After a 10-year run in the limelight, once again there was no major league soccer in the United States.

In 1921—just a year after the founding of what is now the National Football League—the top soccer teams in the United States formed the American Professional Soccer League.

There was, however, something else: a youth soccer boom. Because of Pele and the NASL, millions of youngsters—girls as well as boys—started kicking soccer balls. They formed teams, joined leagues, and went to camps. They discovered the joy of the world's most popular game, and taught their parents about it, too.

At the same time that the NASL was shrinking, youth soccer was growing. So was college soccer. The game was developing from the bottom up, not the top down. Millions of Americans were enjoying soccer on a local level.

And then came the 1994 World Cup. Major League Soccer began two years later. Once again, the world's soccer eyes were focused on the United States.

SOCCER IN THE UNITED STATES TODAY

When the North American Soccer League collapsed, many people thought it signaled the end of soccer in the United States. Of course, that did not happen. In fact, soccer grew even more rapidly than ever.

During the 1980s, the number of young soccer players rose like a rocket. Across the country, boys and girls were learning to love soccer. Some of the early soccer strongholds were places that might be expected, like the Maryland and Virginia suburbs around Washington, D.C., and the warm-weather sports-crazy states of Florida and California.

But soccer also grew rapidly in many other places that might not have been expected. In Dallas, where the NFL Cowboys had always reigned supreme, the number of youth soccer players quickly exceeded the number of football players. In Minnesota, soccer sped past hockey to become the most popular sport, in terms of numbers of youth players. And soccer soon spread to more rural areas. States like Vermont, New Mexico, and Idaho were filled with young girls and boys playing the game.

Soccer fields and goal posts sprouted up where empty lots once stood. Teams needed coaches, so parents took courses to learn how to teach this "new" game. Other adults learned how to be referees. An entire new industry grew up around souvenir patches and pins, used for trading between players on different teams.

The youth players of the 1980s got older and went on to high school. Suddenly, schools started adding soccer to their list of sports. Some states played high school soccer in the fall, some in the spring, a few in the winter, but it was not long before all 50 states had high school championships.

Then the high school players moved on to college. College soccer had been played for years before, but it was always a minor, low-key sport. The first national championship was held in 1959, and for the next 25 years or so it attracted little attention. But then a series of

exciting teams drew attention to the college game. The University of
Connecticut, the University of Indiana, Clemson University, the
University of California at Los Angeles, Duke—the men's title switched
hands many times, back and forth across the country.

In the early 1990s, the first men's college soccer dynasty
emerged. The University of Virginia Cavaliers reeled off four straight
national championships, and they did it using only American players.
They were members of the Atlantic Coast Conference (ACC), widely
admired as the best men's college soccer league in the country. The
ACC featured exciting competition, intense rivalries, and something
new: great stadiums. Virginia, for example, built Klockner Stadium, a
state-of-the-art facility with lush grass and perfect sightlines.

But when it comes to college soccer dynasties, nobody could beat
the University of North Carolina (UNC) Tar Heels women. Also an ACC
team, the Tar Heels under coach Anson Dorrance won an incredible

nine consecutive NCAA championships. Year in and year
out, for almost a decade, no
one could stop UNC. They
won more than 100 straight
games at one point, and
single-handedly put women's
soccer on the map.

UNC players were great
role models for female soccer
players. Women players like
Michelle Akers, Carin
Jennings, and April Heinrichs
became even more famous
when they helped lead the
United States to the first
Women's World Cup championship in China in 1991. The

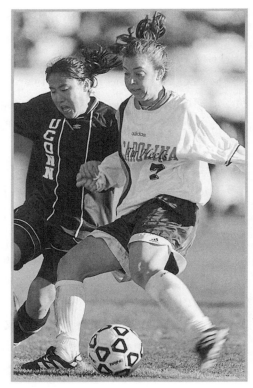

Robin Confer of UNC battles against a
UConn player.

The U.S. Women's Olympic team after winning gold in 1996.

United States beat Norway in front of 60,000 fans. Four years later the Americans finished third, in Sweden. (Norway got revenge.) In 1996, playing in front of home crowds at the Summer Olympics, the U.S. women won the gold medal. (It was the first time women's soccer had ever been played at the Olympics.) Although it has taken the U.S. men's team a long time to gain international respect, American women are already widely viewed as the best in the world.

There is even a women's pro league now, the "W" League. It doesn't get a lot of publicity, and salaries are low, but the "W" league gives young female soccer players something to shoot for. So does the next big event on the women's schedule: the second Women's World Cup, which will be played the summer of 1999 in the United States.

But the biggest story in American soccer is the pros. Major league soccer is back, and it's called . . . Major League Soccer (MLS).

The league's first official game, in April 1996, started with a bang. It was played at Spartan Stadium in San Jose, California. So many people showed up—more than 31,000 in all, which is more than the stadium officially holds—that officials had to keep opening up new sections to hold everyone. Eric Wynalda's spectacular goal led the hometown Clash to a 1-0 victory over D.C. United.

Attendance remained high throughout the season. Fans tooted horns and whistled loudly, just as they do in soccer stadiums around the world. In June, more than 92,000 people packed the Rose Bowl to watch the Los Angeles Galaxy capture a 3–2 shootout win over the Tampa Bay Mutiny.

The MLS is filled with big names. Some come from America, while others are from Europe, South America, and Africa. There is Jorge Campos, the Los Angeles Galaxy's wide-ranging goalkeeper (he's been known to roam all the way past midfield); Roberto Donadoni of the New York/New Jersey MetroStars, a World Cup sensation from Italy; and Carlos Valderrama, the Tampa Bay Mutiny's bushy-haired, brilliant playmaker from Colombia.

Among the top American stars are Alexi Lalas of New England, the unstoppable national team defender; Tab Ramos of the MetroStars, who has spent many years representing the United States; and San Jose's Eric Wynalda, the goal-scorer supreme.

Many rising stars are getting great experience playing in the MLS. Names to watch in the future include Jason Kreis of Dallas, Roy Lassiter of Tampa Bay, Brian McBride of Columbus, and Eddie Pope of D.C.

The first MLS season was capped by a remarkable championship game. No one gave D.C.

Goal-scoring sensation Eric Wynalda.

United much of a chance after they lost their first four games of the year, but they got on track and roared into the finals. MLS Cup '96 was played in Foxboro, Mass., the home of the New England Revolution, in a vicious, driving rainstorm. But the weather did not stop either United or their opponents, the Los Angeles Galaxy.

Los Angeles took a 2-0 lead, and with 17 minutes to play that advantage looked secure. But Tony Sanneh leaped high to head home Mario Etcheverry's cross, and suddenly D.C. was on the move.

With just eight minutes remaining, Shawn Medved attacked. He was a late substitute, but was eager to show he could do the job. Goalkeeper Jorge Campos punched away his first shot, but Medved stayed with the rebound. He pounced on the loose ball and rocketed it home, tying the match 2-2.

Now D.C. United had the momentum. Four minutes into sudden death overtime, Etcheverry blasted a corner kick toward the Galaxy penalty box. Eddie Pope, the speedy 22-year-old, rose to meet the ball, while the wet and tired defenders stood still. Pope drilled a hard header into the back of the net, to give United the incredible come-from-behind victory.

But the best was yet to come. Pope raced toward the D.C. bench and launched himself into a full belly-slide, only to be engulfed by his happy, rain- and mud-drenched teammates. The crowd of nearly 35,000, which had stayed throughout the monsoon, applauded in delight.

The 1997 season brought a dip in attendance, as the league's novelty wore off. However, there was plenty of excitement. Teams that had struggled in the first season, like the Kansas City Wizards and New England Revolution, found themselves in the playoff hunt. The Colorado Rockies, the league's laughingstock its first season, completed a remarkable transformation. They powered their way to the championship game, playing in Washington's RFK Stadium against D.C. United. A capacity crowd of 57,000 braved pouring rain to cheer the home team on.

Alas for the Rockies, their storybook season ended one win short of a title. D.C. United made it two straight championships, this time with a hard-earned 2-1 victory.

TOP AMERICAN PLAYERS

T hough the U.S. national men's and women's team rosters are constantly changing, many players have been with the program long enough to achieve star status. They're the men and women whose names are known around the globe; they're the ones who bring glory to American soccer.

MARCELO BALBOA
Defender

In 1995 Marcelo became the first American player ever to play 100 international games (in soccer terms, that means he earned 100 "caps"). He made the game a memorable occasion, scoring his team's second goal in a 3–2 win over Nigeria. What makes that especially remarkable is that Marcelo is a defender.

But he can score, too. At the 1994 World Cup, against Colombia, he flew in the air and launched a spectacular "bicycle kick" that came within just a few inches of scoring. That World Cup was clearly successful for Marcelo: he was one of five Americans who played every minute of every game. In 1991, he did score on a bicycle kick, getting the winning goal in the opening Gold Cup tournament game against Trinidad and Tobago.

Marcelo was named U.S. Soccer's Male Athlete of the Year twice, in 1992 and '94. The second award was especially impressive. In April 1993 he suffered a major knee injury in a game against Iceland. Some people thought his soccer career was over. But just seven months later, after vigorous rehabilitation, he returned to the field in a match against El Salvador.

Marcelo's first coach was his father, Luis, while growing up in Southern California. Balboa's youth team, Fram-Culver, won the McGuire Cup Under-19 national championship in 1986. Marcelo then played at San Diego State University. After six years in the American Professional Soccer League, he now stars for the MLS's Colorado Rapids.

Best strength: Marcelo Balboa is a smart defender with excellent vision.

PAUL CALIGIURI
Defender

If Paul Caligiuri does nothing for the rest of his soccer life, he will be remembered for one thing. On November 19, 1989, he scored the only goal in a World Cup qualifying game against Trinidad and Tobago. That 1–0 win earned the U.S. national team the right to play in the 1990 tournament, America's first World Cup qualification in 40 years.

But Paul did not rest on his laurels. He scored America's first World Cup goal since 1950 against Czechoslovakia, in that '90 tournament in Italy.

Paul is a very versatile player. He has seen action in back as a sweeper, and in midfield as a flank attacker. That versatility helped him start every match for the United States at both the 1990 and '94 World Cups, as well as the 1988 Olympic Games in South Korea.

Paul was also one of the first Americans to play overseas. He helped the German team Hansa Rostock win the Oberliga championship, which earned them promotion into the First Division (Bundesliga) for the 1991–92 season. In 1995, in his first game for St. Pauli, he was named one of the top players of the week in the entire German league.

Paul was coached by his father, Bob, as a youth player in California. His West Coast roots run deep. He played college soccer at the University of California at Los Angeles (UCLA), and was captain in 1985 when they won the NCAA Division I championship. He even made a guest appearance on the television show "Beverly Hills 90210" in 1994, playing himself.

But Paul is interested in what's happening in the rest of America, too. In 1995, when he signed with the L.A. Salsa of the USISL, he donated part of his salary to the victims of the Oklahoma City bombing.

Best strength: Paul Caligiuri's versatility makes him an asset anywhere.

THOMAS DOOLEY
Midfielder

It's not often that a player has to learn a new language to play on his own national team. But that's what happened to Thomas Dooley. And everyone connected with American soccer was delighted.

Thomas's father was a U.S. Army veteran who married a German woman. He was raised in Germany, and while he always thought of

himself as German, he also thought of America—a country he had never visited.

Thomas first played professional soccer in Germany in 1985, for a third division team called Homburg. He worked his way up the German soccer ladder, and in 1991 had his best year. As a defensive midfielder, he was the star of the FC Kaiserslautern defense, and also scored four goals. His team won the German championship.

Someone in the U.S. Soccer office learned that Thomas had an American father, and knew that because he had never played for the German national team, he was eligible to play for America. This was a great opportunity for Thomas, and in 1992 he became a U.S. citizen.

That same year he joined the U.S. national team, and played every minute of the U.S. Cup. He led America to the championship—and learned enough English to communicate with his teammates off the field as well as on.

The following year he was named U.S. Soccer Male Athlete of the Year. He started 17 matches for the national team in 1993. On Dec. 18, when the United States played his native Germany, he served as captain.

In 1994 Thomas was the only American midfielder to play every minute of every World Cup game. Despite suffering a stress fracture in his ankle in 1995, he continued to star for his adopted country. In 1996 he scored the winning goal in America's win over Guatemala, part of the qualifying process for the '98 World Cup in France.

Best strength: Thomas Dooley's German League experience is invaluable on the U.S. squad.

BRAD FRIEDEL
Goalkeeper

If one of the qualities of a good goalkeeper is long reach, then Brad Friedel should be one of the best in the world. At six-feet, four-inches, he's got an enormous wingspan. Added to this are his other assets—great reflexes, superb jumping ability, strength, and fearlessness.

Fearless is exactly what Brad is for the U.S. national team. In fact, he's been a spectacular athlete all his life, going all the way back to high school in Lakewood, Ohio, where he earned 11 varsity letters in soccer, basketball, and tennis. Because he was an All-State basketball player, he was invited to try out as a walk-on for the UCLA Bruins basketball team in 1990.

But Brad decided to stick with soccer, and UCLA (and American) fans are glad he did. In 1990 he led the Bruins to the NCAA Division I championship, saving two penalty kicks in two shootout games along the way. *Soccer America* magazine named him Freshman of the Year.

As a junior in 1993, he won the Hermann Trophy, given to the top college soccer player. He had started all 61 of UCLA's games over three years, and decided to leave school to pursue a pro career. However, he had difficulty getting a work permit in England, and ended up playing with Broendby of Denmark and then Galatasaray of Turkey, winner of 10 Turkish championships. When the MLS was formed in 1996, Galatasaray loaned him to the Columbus Crew.

Brad's national team career did not start out as well as his high school and college careers. Coach Bora Milutinovic named him backup keeper to Tony Meola for the 1994 World Cup, but did not play him at all. This was a controversial decision. Many soccer observers thought Brad was quicker and had better range than Tony. Tony, however, had much more international experience than Brad.

Brad did get to play for the Olympic team in 1992. He also joined the national team for Copa America, when he saved two out of three penalty kicks in a quarterfinal shootout victory over Mexico.

When Steve Sampson took over as national team coach in 1995, he named Brad his top goalkeeper. It's not easy getting on the field as a goalie—only one is allowed at a time—but as the 1998 World Cup neared, it looked like Brad might be number one in the U.S. nets for years to come.

Best strength: Brad Friedel has excellent reach and range.

JOHN HARKES
Midfielder

There is no higher honor in American soccer than to be named national team captain. That honor belongs to New Jersey native, John Harkes.

He started 13 games for the United States in 1996 as a midfielder, and led the team with five assists. A 1990 and '94 World Cup veteran, he played 270 minutes in '94, including every minute of every first-round game. He was named co-Most Valuable Player in the 1995 Copa America, having led the U.S. team to the semifinals. John was also named Most Valuable Player of U.S. Cup '92, when he scored two goals for the championship U.S. team. John's national team career dates back to 1987, when he debuted as a 20-year-old.

But John's accomplishments don't end with the national team. In 1996 he was named captain of D.C. United, which won the first MLS championship. Before the MLS, he starred in the tough English League, playing with West Ham United and Sheffield Wednesday of the Premier Division, and Derby County of the First Division. With Sheffield, he made history not once, but twice. In April 1993 he became the first American ever to score a goal in the Coca-Cola League Cup Final, and the next month was the first American ever to play in an FA Cup Final.

British fans have admired John ever since 1990, when he scored the English League's Goal of the Year. It was a 35-yard rocket into the upper left corner against goalkeeper Peter Shilton, England's former captain and all-time appearance leader.

John was a teammate of U.S. national team goalkeeper Tony Meola at Kearny High School, and of Tab Ramos during their youth soccer days. He played college soccer at the University of Virginia. In 1987, as a junior, he was named both Missouri Athletic Club Player of the Year

for the United States, and Atlantic Coast Conference Player of the Year.
Best strength: John Harkes is not flashy, but his consistent leadership is exactly what the U.S. team needs.

COBI JONES
Midfielder

Dreadlocks flying, slender body streaking upfield, Cobi Jones is one of the most recognizable of all U.S. players. But it takes more than looks to get on the soccer field. Cobi has talent, too.

The midfielder is one of the U.S. national team's all-time assist leaders. He played in every game of the 1994 World Cup, after starring at the '92 Olympics. Coaches like his speed, dribbling skills, and ability to dish out assists.

Cobi was one of the first stars of the MLS. Playing with the Los Angeles Galaxy in 1996, his seven goals and four assists helped the Galaxy reach the league's first championship game.

Cobi came to American pro soccer from England (where he played with Coventry City) and Brazil (where he signed with first division team Vasco da Gama). He played college soccer at the University of California at Los Angeles, not far from his boyhood home in Westlake Village, California. At UCLA he was named to the All-Far West team for three consecutive years.

Best strength: Cobi Jones is a quick, smooth-dribbling assist man.

KASEY KELLER
Goalkeeper

At six-foot, two-inches and 180 pounds, Kasey Keller is another in a long line of impressive American goalkeepers. The Olympia, Washington, native has not received as much national team playing time as Tony Meola or Brad Friedel, but when he gets the call he comes through. During qualifying games for World Cup '98, for example, Kasey shut out both Guatemala and Trinidad and Tobago.

(pictured in center)

In 1995, during the Copa America tournament, he helped shut out Argentina 3–0—one of the biggest wins in U.S. soccer history. Kasey is no stranger to shutouts. His 4–0 whitewashing of Mexico in U.S. Cup '95 was the biggest margin of victory ever for the United States over Mexico.

Kasey's U.S. national team career extends back to 1989, when he starred on the Under-20 team that finished fourth at the World Youth Championship in Saudi Arabia. In honor of his play, he was named winner of the prestigious Silver Ball Award, given to the second of three outstanding tournament players. The following year Kasey backed up Tony Meola on the 1990 World Cup squad.

Kasey started his professional career with Millwall of the English First Division. The team's fans voted him Most Valuable Player in 1993. Moving on to Leicester City of the English Premier Division, he established himself as one of the best keepers in that soccer-mad country.

Kasey played college soccer at the University of Portland (UP). As a freshman in 1988 he led the UP Pilots to the NCAA Division I final four. Two years later he was named to the All-America first team, and was a top vote-getter for both the Hermann Trophy and Missouri Athletic Club Award.

Best strength: Kasey Keller has complete and utter command of his penalty box.

ALEXI LALAS
Defender

Who has not seen—or at least heard of—Alexi Lalas?

With his scraggly hair and red goatee, Alexi was easily the most recognizable player on the U.S. 1994 World Cup team. He proved you do not have to be a forward to get all the glory. His bone-crunching tackles and out-of-danger heading helped lead the United States to a 1–1–1 record as the host country.

But even if you didn't watch soccer, you knew the name Alexi Lalas. He made television appearances on all the late-night talk shows. And as a guitarist and singer in the rock group The Gypsies, at times it seemed as if he was everywhere.

But despite his looks and outside interests, Alexi is first and foremost a soccer player. *U.S. Soccer* named him 1995 Male Athlete of the Year, and journalists voted him one of 11 players to the 1995 All-Copa America team. In 1993 Alexi was the only American selected to play in an important charity match in Italy. The game pitted the "Christmas All-Stars" against AC Milan.

In 1994 he signed with Padova. That made him the first American-born player in the modern era to compete in Italy's *Serie A*, considered the top soccer league in the world. Italian fans immediately took to his take-no-prisoners style of defense. They also liked his eagerness to go forward on penalty kicks, and score with his head.

But when the MLS began in 1996, Alexi came home to America. He signed with the New England Revolution. In Februrary 1998 he was traded to the New York/New Jersey Metro Stars.

Alexi was born and grew up in suburban Detroit. In 1987, while at Cranbrook Kingswood High School, he was named Michigan Player of the Year. He also captained his high school ice hockey team to the state title. He continued his hockey career while at Rutgers University (and even led the team in scoring in 1989). However, soccer was his true love. He was the unanimous choice for college player of the year as a senior in 1991, winning both the Hermann Trophy and Missouri Athletic Club Award.

Best strength: Alexi Lalas is best known for his bone-crunching tackles and great air game.

ROY LASSITER
Striker

As one of the fastest players on the U.S. national team, Roy Lassiter has always had potential. Only recently, however, has that potential started to unleash itself.

In December 1996 Roy scored the winning goal in America's 2–1 victory over Costa Rica, a must-win game that lifted them into the final round of regional qualifying for World Cup '98.

Roy also was a star for the Tampa Bay Mutiny during the first MLS season. In fact, he led the entire league with 27 goals.

Yet it took a while for Roy to reach that level of stardom. His youth club, Raleigh (N.C.) United lost in the McGuire Cup (Under-19) national finals in 1989. Roy finished third in NCAA Division I scoring as a senior, notching 22 goals for North Carolina State University. But a series of injuries and brushes with the law led him to play professionally first in Costa Rica, a country not well known for soccer. He then moved on to Genoa, in Italy's second division (*Serie B*). Because of some of his past problems, U.S. Soccer officials were hesitant to take a chance on Roy. But they did, and finally—at nearly 30 years old—he seems to be coming into his own.

Best strength: Roy Lassiter is one of the fastest players on the U.S. national team.

TONY MEOLA
Goalkeeper

Though he is no longer the U.S. national team goalkeeper, Tony Meola's place in history is secure. He captained the 1994 World Cup team, and was one of only five players to play every minute of every game. Four years earlier, at just 21, he was the U.S. keeper in Italy, during America's first World Cup appearance in 40 years.

Internationally, Tony earned 30 shutouts in 89 appearances.

His college career at the University of Virginia was highlighted by his selection in 1989 as both Hermann Trophy winner and Missouri Athletic Club Player of the Year.

Tony's athletic career has several interesting highlights. At Kearny (N.J.) High School, he was a teammate of John Harkes. Occasionally, the coach let Tony out of the goal, and he proved himself a fierce offensive player, too. He was glad to be scoring goals, not saving them.

After high school he was drafted as a center fielder by the New York Yankees, but decided to stick with soccer. However, when the 1994 World Cup ended he decided to try another sport. He signed with the New York Jets as a place kicker, but eventually was cut and went back to soccer. Today Tony Meola tends nets for the New York/New Jersey MetroStars of Major League Soccer.

Best strength: Tony Meola's many years of international experience make him an excellent defensive leader.

TAB RAMOS
Midfielder

Playmaker is not a role many soccer players can handle. A playmaker is a midfielder who, because of his combination of skills, stamina, vision, intelligence, and experience, is able to create opportunities for everyone else on the field.

But playmaking is what Tab Ramos does best. And that is why he is known as one of America's best soccer players, ever.

Tab has soccer in his blood. His father, Julian, played professionally in Uruguay, and Tab grew up in soccer-crazy Kearny, N.J. (He was a youth soccer teammate of John Harkes.) In 1983, playing for St. Benedict's Prep in Newark, he was named High School Player of the Year.

Tab drew raves at North Carolina State University, where he was named first team All-America, and ended his senior year as the Atlantic Coast Conference's top scorer.

He was one of the first American players to succeed in Europe. He first signed with Figueres, then moved to Betis, both second division teams in Spain. Next came a stint with Nuevo León of the Mexican first division. In 1996 he was the first player signed to an MLS contract. His new team was the New York/New Jersey MetroStars. They play their home games at Giants Stadium, just a few miles from Kearny. Tab's soccer journey had brought him home again.

While playing professionally abroad, Ramos made frequent trips back to America for years, to play for the U.S. national team. He was also a member of both the 1988 U.S. Olympic team and the small-sided squad that finished third at the first-ever FIFA World Championship for Five-a-Side Football in the Netherlands, in 1989.

Tab started all three games at the 1990 World Cup in Italy, and a few months later scored against AC Milan in an international all-star charity match.

The 1994 World Cup started out well for Tab. He served a perfect through pass to Ernie Stewart, who scored the game-winner against Colombia in first-round action. But a brutal elbow to the head fractured Tab's skull late in the first half of the second-round match against Brazil. Some observers said that could have been a turning point in the 1–0 U.S. loss that eliminated them from further competition.

Tab became the U.S. all-time assist leader in 1996, but late in the year suffered a tear in his left knee ligament. That kept him out of action for most of 1997. But his experience and skill were not harmed, and he was expected to regain his key position on the U.S. national team by the end of qualifying for World Cup '98.

Best strength: Tab Ramos is a skillful, smart, and visionary playmaker.

CLAUDIO REYNA
Midfielder

The fourth and youngest member of U.S. Soccer's fearsome New Jersey connection (John Harkes, Tony Meola, and Tab Ramos are the other three) is Claudio Reyna. He, too, is a graduate of St. Benedict's Prep, where he was a two-time *Parade* Magazine National Player of the Year, and Gatorade Player of the Year. During that time, St. Benedict won two straight state championships, and put together a 47-game winning streak.

Claudio's winning ways continued at the University of Virginia. During his years there the Cavaliers captured three straight NCAA Division I titles (1991, '92, and '93). Claudio picked up a host of honors, including Missouri Athletic Club Player of the Year (1992 and '93), Soccer America Player of the Year (1992 and '93), Soccer America Freshman of the Year (1991), and three selections to the All-America first team.

Claudio left Virginia and went right to the top. He signed with Bayer Leverkusen of Germany's Bundesliga (first division) in 1994.

However, 1994 was not perfect for Claudio. He made the World Cup team—in fact, he was the youngest member—but did not play at all, due to a hamstring injury. He had hoped to build on his previous international experience. In 1992 he helped America to a 1-1-1 record at the 1992 Olympic Games in Barcelona, playing every minute and assisting on two goals from his midfield spot. He was the youngest member of that squad, too.

Claudio's most productive day in a national team uniform came during U.S. Cup '95. He scored one goal and assisted on two more, in a historic 4-0 defeat of Mexico.

With the 1998 World Cup looming, the world will hear plenty more from Claudio Reyna.

Best strength: Claudio Reyna adds an offensive dimension to any midfield.

ERNIE STEWART
Striker

Like Thomas Dooley, Ernie Stewart took a strange path to the U.S. national team. His father, Ernie, was a U.S. Air Force veteran and former football player who married a noted Dutch sprinter. Ernie lived in California between the ages of 2 and 7, but played no soccer there.

However, when he moved to the Netherlands, he picked up the Dutch national game, and quickly became a star. At 17, Stewart signed his first professional contract, and soon made it to the first division with NAC Breda. His 50-plus goals in Dutch soccer brought him to the attention of U.S. Soccer officials. Since he had never represented the Netherlands in international competition, he was eligible to compete for the United States.

Ernie played for his "new" country at U.S. Cups '92 and '93. During World Cup '94, he started all four matches for the United States. His game-winning goal against Colombia pushed the U.S. into the second round.

Ernie's ball-handling ability and speed make him a valuable asset, whether in the Dutch league or with the U.S. national team.

Best strength: Ernie Stewart is a quick, sure dribbler.

ERIC WYNALDA
Striker

This Southern California native was named U.S. Soccer Male Athlete of the Year in 1996, the same time he became America's all-time leading scorer (27 goals). Eric Wynalda's value is shown by this statistic: Through 1996, the United States won 18 games, tied 3, and lost only 2 in which he scored. But leading the American scoring parade is not the only way Eric finishes first.

He was on the World Cup squad in 1990, playing in two out of three games, but made his real mark four years later. In the very first game the U.S. team played, against Switzerland in the Silverdome, Eric laced a spectacular 28-yard free kick into the upper left corner. That goal earned the United States a crucial 1–1 tie. He went on to play in three other World Cup matches, too.

Eric registered another first in 1996. He scored the first goal in Major League Soccer history when the San Jose Clash defeated D.C. United 1–0.

And he was the first American-born player to break into the Bundesliga (German first division) in 1992. His debut with FC Saarbruecken was explosive. He scored 9 goals in his first 10 games, proving that Americans can indeed play in the top leagues anywhere.

Eric's college career spanned three years at San Diego State University. He played youth soccer with national team teammate Cobi Jones. His father, Dave, played football at Princeton University.

Best strength: Eric Wynalda has a knack for scoring key goals.

MICHELLE AKERS
Striker

Michelle Akers's list of accomplishments is nearly as long as she is tall. The five-foot, ten-inch forward is the U.S. women's national team all-time leading scorer, putting the ball in the net at nearly a goal-a-game pace for more than 100 international matches. She started all five matches during the 1996 Olympic Games—the first time women's soccer was a medal sport—and scored a crucial goal in the United States's 2–1 semifinal victory over Norway. She was named Most Valuable Player at the 1996 U.S. Women's Cup, and Most Valuable Player of the 1994 CONCACAF qualifying tournament for the 1995 world championship.

Earlier in her illustrious career, Michelle was the leading goal scorer at the inaugural FIFA Women's World Championship, held in

1991 in China. She tallied 10 goals—including five in one game—to win the Golden Boot Award. She also received the Silver Ball Award, given to that tournament's second best player. Her performance in China helped lead the United States to its first world soccer championship, male or female. U.S. Soccer named Michelle Female Athlete of the Year in both 1990 and '91.

At the University of Central Florida in Orlando, where Michelle was a four-time All-America selection, she won the first-ever women's Hermann Trophy, given to the top college soccer player in America. After graduation, she played three seasons with the Tyreso Football Club in Sweden.

Perhaps most remarkable about Michelle is that for several years in the mid-'90s she suffered from Epstein-Barr syndrome, a long-term disease that causes intense fatigue. Still, she played soccer—and scored, and won awards.

Best strength: Michelle Akers has a nose for the goal.

JOY FAWCETT
Defender

Joy Fawcett is a workhorse. She started and played every minute of the United States's five matches at the 1996 Olympic Games, and was one of only two women to see action in every minute of the United States's six games at the 1995 FIFA Women's World Championship in Sweden.

But Joy does more than simply work hard. A defender, she also goes forward. She earned the assist on Tiffeny Milbrett's goal against China that clinched a gold medal for America at the '96 Olympics. She was named U.S. Soccer's Female Athlete of the Year as far back as 1988, a great accomplishment for a defender whose play often gets overlooked.

At the University of California at Berkeley, Joy was a three-time All-America selection. Her college connection continued in 1993, when she was named the first women's soccer coach at the University of California at Los Angeles.

Best strength: Joy often makes slashing runs upfield from her defensive position.

JULIE FOUDY
Midfielder

One of the longest-serving members of the U.S. women's national team, Julie Foudy served as cocaptain of the gold medal-winning team at the 1996 Olympic Games. She started and played every minute of the United States's five games in that historic tournament.

Five years earlier, Julie was on the field for every second in China, where the United States captured the first-ever FIFA Women's World Championship. Her national team debut came in 1988, when she was just 16 years old.

Julie played college soccer at Stanford University. She was named to the All-America team four years in a row, and *Soccer America* magazine honored her twice: as Freshman of the Year in 1989, and Player of the Year two years later. The *Los Angeles Times,* near her hometown of Mission Viejo, California, named Julie its soccer player of the decade for the 1980s.

In 1994 Julie played professional soccer in Sweden with the Tyreso Football Club. Her teammates included fellow national team members Michelle Akers, Mary Harvey, and Kristine Lilly. Sandwiched around her European experience were two seasons with the Sacramento Storm, which in 1993 and '95 won the California State Amateur championship.

Best strength: Julie Foudy has excellent vision and distribution skills.

CARIN GABARRA
Striker

Carin Gabarra, who has played on such notable teams as the 1996 Olympic gold medalists, the 1991 FIFA world champions, and the bronze medal FIFA world championship squad in 1995, is the third highest scorer in U.S. women's soccer history (she trails only Michelle Akers and Mia Hamm). The U.S. Soccer Federation has honored her twice as Female Athlete of the Year, in 1987 and '92. Perhaps her biggest honor came in 1991,

when FIFA awarded her the Golden Ball, as outstanding player of the first Women's World Championship. She scored six goals in that tournament.

A four-time All-America selection at the University of California–Santa Barbara, Carin was voted Woman Athlete of the Decade there in 1987. Her jersey was retired prior to the FIFA World Championship in 1991.

Carin's club team, Ajax of Southern California, won the U.S. Women's Amateur Cup in 1992 and '93. In 1993 she was drafted by L.A. United of the Continental Indoor Soccer League—a men's league. That same year she was named the first women's soccer coach at the U.S. Naval Academy in Annapolis, Maryland.

Carin's husband, Jim Gabarra, is a former member of the U.S. national team.

Best strength: Carin holds onto the ball well in tight situations.

MIA HAMM
Striker

In 1997 Mia Hamm made history, becoming the first four-time winner of the U.S. Soccer Athlete of the Year Award. No other athlete had ever done that, and she did it in four *consecutive* years.

Mia, generally considered the best all-around woman player in the world, scores many goals from her forward position. But she is also a team leader in assists. Her versatility extends to several positions. During the FIFA Women's World Championship in 1995, she played forward, midfielder, and even took a stint in goal.

Mia is also courageous. She sprained her ankle against Sweden in the first round of the 1996 Olympic Games, but fought through the injury to lead the United States to victories over Norway in the semi-finals, then China in the championship match.

Her awards include Most Valuable Player of U.S. Women's Cup '95, and selection by fans as the Most Valuable Player of Chiquita Cup '94.

She was the youngest member of the women's world championship team in 1991, starting five of six games at the age of 19, and scoring twice. She is also the youngest woman ever to play with the U.S. national team, taking the field at just 15.

Mia is a two-time winner of both the Hermann Trophy and Missouri Athletic Club Award, the two top honors in collegiate soccer. At the University of North Carolina (UNC) she helped win four straight NCAA championships, and was named to the All-America team three times. When she completed her college career as the Atlantic Coast Conference's all-time leader in goals (103), assists (72), and points (278), UNC retired her number (19).

Best strength: Mia is a versatile player, well skilled all over the field.

KRISTINE LILLY
Midfielder

Quietly, without much fanfare, Kristine Lilly has emerged as one of the most consistent, most talented—and *best*—women players in the world.

The Wilton, Connecticut, native makes things happen from her midfield position. Among the things she has made happen are winning the first-ever FIFA World Championship in 1991; a third-place finish for the United States at the same tournament in 1995, and a gold medal at the 1996 Olympic Games.

Kristine was named U.S. Soccer's 1993 Female Athlete of the Year. In 1991, while at the University of North Carolina, she won the Hermann Trophy as the top college player of the year. The following year she was runnerup. She also was a four-time All-America selection. In her honor, UNC—where she won four consecutive NCAA championships—retired her number (15) in 1994.

In 1994 Kristine played for Tyreso Football Club in Sweden, along with national team teammates Michelle Akers, Julie Foudy, and Mary Harvey. The following year she moved over to men's soccer, playing with the Washington Warthogs of the Continental Indoor Soccer League. The team was coached by Jim Gabarra, husband of national team forward Carin Gabarra.

Best strength: Kristine Lilly controls a game with her vision and touch.

THE U.S. NATIONAL TEAMS

The U.S. Soccer Federation (USSF) sponsors seven "U.S. national teams." Five are for males—the men's full national team, Under-23 (Olympic), Under-20, Under-17, and Futsal (five-a-side)—while two are for women—women's full national team and Under-20.

There are also three "developmental" teams—boys Under-18, boys Under-16, and girls Under-16. These teams do not participate in official international competition, but do play games and scrimmages against international opponents, usually club teams.

All national teams compete under the direction of the USSF. The younger teams serve as a "feeder" system for the full men's and women's teams.

MEN'S NATIONAL TEAM

This is the "flagship" team, the one people think of first when they hear the words "U.S. team." It is the team that competes for the World Cup, and it consists of the top male players in the country.

The men's national team has competed in five World Cups. The team was invited to the first, in 1930; qualified for the 1934, 1950, and 1990 World Cups, and in 1994 was automatically invited as the host nation. (For details on America's World Cup accomplishments, see the "World Cup" chapter.)

Since 1990, the men's national team has been near the top in the CONCACAF (North America, Central America, and Caribbean) region. Before 1990, they lost more games than they won in the region, but since, the U.S. national team has won four times as often as they have lost.

In 1997, the men's national team went through the qualifying process for the 1998 World Cup in France. In mid-November, thanks to a 0–0 tie in Mexico and a 3–0 win in Canada a week later, the United States earned one of the 32 coveted spots.

The men's national team also hosts the U.S. Cup, a four-team, six-game international tournament held every year against top teams. The national team also stays sharp by playing "friendly" matches against a series of international opponents. The men's team has been ranked as high as 14 in FIFA's world rankings.

WOMEN'S NATIONAL TEAM

The women's national team is the United States's most successful team. They won the first Women's World Cup in 1991 in China. They also captured the first women's Olympic soccer championship, defeating China 2–1 in the finals at the 1996 Atlanta Games before a Stanford Stadium crowd of 76,481. In 1995 the women placed third at the World Cup, falling 1–0 to archrival and eventual champion, Norway, in the semifinals.

U.S. Women's National Team winning the first Women's World Cup in 1991 in China.

The Americans' next goal is to win the third Women's World Cup, which will be played in the United States in 1999.

The women's national team was formed in 1985. Since that time, the team has won more than 100 games, including a 21–1–2 record in 1996.

MEN'S OLYMPIC TEAM

Although the women's national team also competes in the Olympics, things are different at the men's level. According to Olympic rules, men's competition is limited to players under 23, although three over-age (called "wild card") players were permitted in the 1996 Games. Consequently, the U.S. men's Olympic team is also the national Under-23 team. Most members of the U.S. Under-23 team play professionally, either in the MLS or abroad.

Overall, the U.S. Olympic team's results are not good. Before 1992 (the year the Under-23 team became the Olympic team), the United States had a record of 2–10–4, spread across the 1924, 1928, 1936, 1948, 1952, 1956, 1972, 1984, and 1988 Games.

After the changeover to Under-23 teams, the U.S. record has been 7–3–2.

MEN'S UNDER-20 TEAM

The U.S. Under-20 men's team qualified as one of three CONCACAF teams for the 1997 FIFA World Championships, held in Malaysia in 1997. Uruguay eliminated the United States in the second round, 3–0. It was the third time the Americans reached the second round of the Under-20 tournament. They finished fourth in 1989, and eighth in 1993. That '93 tournament is remembered for the United States's phenomenal 6–0 opening game win over Europe's top seed, Turkey. One FIFA official called it "the most extraordinary result in the history of the tournament."

Despite a 2–1 record in CONCACAF qualifying, the United States failed to qualify for the 1995 World Championship in Nigeria.

WOMEN'S UNDER-20 TEAM

The U.S. Under-20 women's team has been active since 1992. Their first match came at an international tournament in France. The Americans finished with a record of 1–2–1. Yet just one year later, the U.S. Under-20 won an International Women's Tournament also in France, finishing undefeated with wins over Russia, Sweden, France, and Denmark.

More than a dozen of the current women's national team pool members have competed as Under-20s.

BOYS UNDER-17 TEAM

In 1996 the U.S. boys Under-17 team qualified for their seventh consecutive FIFA World Championship. The United States and Australia are the only countries to qualify for every Under-17 World Championship since the tournament began in 1985.

The Americans' highest finish came in 1991, when they placed fifth. Highlights included a victory over the host country, Italy, in the opening match, and a 1–0 win over Argentina. In 1993 the U.S. Under–17 team reached the quarterfinals in Japan before falling to Poland, 3–0.

In other World Championship appearances, the American boys placed 12th in 1985 in China, 14th in 1987 in Canada, 10th in 1989 in Scotland, and 15th in 1995 in Ecuador.

MEN'S FUTSAL (FIVE-A-SIDE) TEAM

The U.S. Futsal national team (formerly called the U.S. national indoor team) turned in the best American finish ever at any world championship by placing second at the Second FIFA Indoor Five-a-Side World Championship in Hong Kong in 1992. Brazil defeated the United States 4–1 in the final match, to win their second straight five-a-side world title.

The U.S. team finished third at the first indoor championship held in 1989 in the Netherlands. This was the first medal in American soccer history ever won in a major international competition. It was also the first time a U.S. men's team reached the second round of any world championship competition since the 1930 World Cup.

The U.S. Futsal national team was eliminated in the opening round of the 1996 World Championship in Spain.

Part III:
Playing
the Game

POSITIONS

Believe it or not, soccer has not always been played with one to three forwards, three to five midfielders, and three to four defenders (plus, of course, a goalkeeper). In the early days, in fact, there were no clear positions at all. A soccer match in the 1800s probably looked very much like one of today's children's games with six-year-olds, with players swarming all around the ball.

But as rules were made, form and structure emerged. Teams slowly organized themselves into positions. A keeper was needed to protect the goal, one or two players stayed back on defense to assist the keeper, and one or two more stationed themselves around the middle of the field (they became known as "midfielders"). The rest considered themselves attackers or "forwards."

The first major formation was called the "WM" system. It was called that because, when you looked at a diagram of a soccer field with the attacking goal at top and the defending goal at bottom, the players spread themselves out in the shape of a "W" in the offensive half of the field, and an "M" on defense. In the offensive half there was a left wing, center forward, and right wing; two insides played a bit behind them. Further back were two players spread across midfield, while all the way back were three defenders.

Over the years the emphasis switched from offense to defense. First there were four defenders; some teams even used five. Franz Beckenbauer of Germany invented the role of "sweeper"—a player

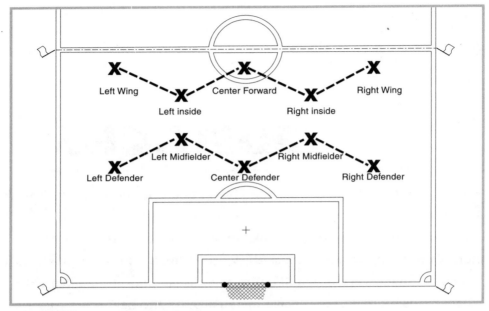

Note: Defenders are also called fullbacks.

who started out behind the other defenders and "swept up" anyone or any ball that got through. After the sweeper won the ball, he or she became an attacker and started upfield.

Three players dribbling up front made things crowded, so gradually the forward line dwindled to two, then just one, player. The name of the forward changed to "front runner." Meanwhile, teams realized that whoever controlled midfield controlled the game, so that area became filled with four or five players on each team.

Keep in mind when reading the following section on positions that there is no right or wrong way to set up players on the field. Soccer is not like baseball, where you definitely need a pitcher, catcher, first baseman, and so on. Different coaches use different soccer lineups or "formations," depending on the strengths and weaknesses of their own players and those on the other team; the size of the field; the weather, etc. One of the great things about soccer is its flexibility, and that extends to the idea of positions.

GOALKEEPER

This is the one position every team must have. The job of the goal-keeper, also called "goalie" or "keeper," is to keep the ball out of the goal. The goalkeeper is special: He or she is the only player allowed to use hands, and the only one wearing a different color jersey.

Goalkeepers should have quick reflexes, and be able to think quickly, too. A keeper should be a leader; he or she must often shout instructions to teammates about who to cover and where to move. A keeper does not have to be a giant, but should be tall enough to cover the goal mouth.

A keeper also needs foot skills. In modern soccer, goalies cannot pick up the ball except if it has been shot; if a teammate makes a pass backward, goalies must play the ball with their feet like regular "field players." More and more, today's keepers are looking like the other 10 players on the field. Jorge Campos of Mexico and the Los Angeles Galaxy, for example, has been known to come up as far as midfield to knock a ball away.

DEFENDERS

Defenders are mainly responsible for protecting the goal—tackling balls from attackers, preventing and intercepting shots—but that is not their only role. As soon as they win the ball, they become offensive players, so they should also be thought of as the players who begin an attack.

The "sweeper" is the player who picks up any ball or player who gets through everyone else; he or she usually plays behind all the other defenders. The "left back" and "right back" guard the outsides (also known as flanks); they mark either "man-to-man" (picking up a particular player) or "zone" (guarding a particular area of the field). The "stopper" is the defender who plays farthest upfield, in the center of the field; he or she is the first line of defense.

The key qualities for defenders are physical and mental toughness, intelligence (to know where the ball is going to be played next), heading ability, and speed (to race back to protect the goal).

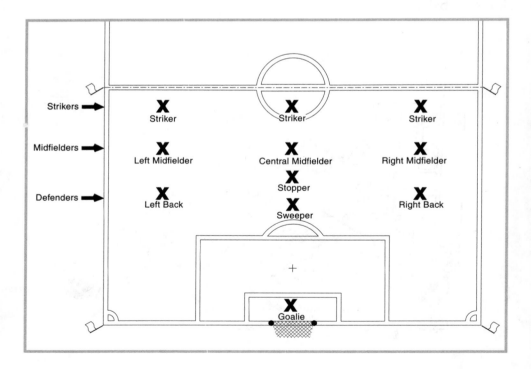

Many defenders enjoy the position because they like the pressure, and because they are able to play while seeing most of the field in front of them.

MIDFIELDERS

Teams may play with three, four, or five midfielders. So there may be one, two, or three "central midfielders," along with a "left midfielder" and "right midfielder." If there is more than one central midfielder, they play in front of and behind each other, rather than side by side. That way, they will not get in each other's way.

In the beginning, goalkeepers wore caps to distinguish themselves from field players. In 1913, they began wearing different color jerseys. Until 1982, however, they could wear only green, yellow, or white.

(Midfielders must think about offense and defense equally.) They are responsible for stopping the other team's attack before it gets near their goal, and for starting their own team's attack at the goal. They must be able to distribute (pass) the ball well, because midfield tends to get crowded; they must be able to go forward, to help with the attack (and receive passes), then run back hard and play defense if they lose the ball.

The key qualities for midfielders are stamina (they do a lot of running), vision (to be able to find open teammates, and switch fields with passes), and ball control skills.

FORWARDS

Forwards are also known as "strikers," "offensive players," or "front runners." Their main job is to finish the attack with a shot on goal, and to keep pressure on the other team so that their own defenders and keeper do not have to face too many shots.

However, forwards are also defensive players. As soon as they lose the ball, they are expected to work hard to get it back.

The key qualities for forwards are speed, good dribbling, and shooting ability.

SKILLS

DRIBBLING

Dribbling is one of the most important skills in soccer. You dribble for many reasons: To get the ball upfield, to beat an opponent, to get in position to take a shot, and to hold the ball because you do not have an open teammate. A player who can dribble well is valuable to any team. And dribbling well means using both feet—don't rely on your strong foot only.

When dribbling, it is important to keep the ball close to you. About two to three feet ahead is good. Any closer and you'll trip over it; any farther away, and you will lose control.

Use the front part of the foot when dribbling, touching the ball near the inside or outside of the foot. Keep your head up as much as possible, so you can see where you are going and what is happening on the rest of the field. Your arms should be slightly out, for balance, not like a windmill, but not down at your sides either.

A good dribbler knows how to change speeds and direction. If you dribble at the same speed and in the same direction all the time, a defender has an easy time taking the ball from you. As you get older, you can add body fakes. There are lots of ways to fake out your opponent when you are dribbling. Stepping over the ball, pulling it back behind you to your other foot, and slowing down before speeding up are just three.

Drills

- Follow the leader (in threes). Everyone can have a soccer ball *or* just the leader can have a ball *or* just the second player. The important thing is to follow whatever the leader does. If he cuts the ball to the left, you do too. If she speeds up into open space, you do the same. Of course, keep the ball close at all times.
- You can also dribble around cones. If you hit a cone with the ball, it "melts," and you get a point. The player with the fewest points at the end of the drill wins.
- In another drill, players line up on the sideline. At one whistle, everyone starts dribbling across the field. On two whistles, everyone stops the ball dead. On three whistles, everyone reverses direction. This is good for learning different moves, and changes of speed and direction.
- Another drill has everyone get into pairs, but only one player in each pair has a ball. The player with the ball dribbles at the one who does not, trying to get past the defender using body fakes, and changes of speed and direction.

Relay races are also lots of fun. You can do this in pairs, with a different variation each time. One time you can dribble out to a line and back as fast as you can. The next time you can dribble the ball with the inside of the foot only; the next time, with the outside of the foot. Then you can dribble out, and when you reach the far line, change directions by stepping on top of the ball to stop it. The next time you dribble, you must use only your weak foot.

Another drill starts with four players in a square 20 yards apart. Each player starts on the outside of one of the sides of the square. On the whistle, everyone dribbles quickly toward the middle. The idea is to control the ball when the three other players all meet in the middle. Once you get through the crowd, speed up again to reach the opposite line.

CONTROLLING

Once upon a time coaches used to talk about "trapping" the ball, but "controlling" it is a better word. "Trapping" meant stopping the ball dead; "controlling" it means that you have the ball under control, but it is still moving. Whatever you call it, the idea is the same: You are in charge of the ball no matter how much pressure is around.

To control a soccer ball, you must keep your weight low by bending at the knees. The lower you are to the ground, the easier it is to move around and shift direction. You can control the ball using either the inside or outside of your foot, as well as your thigh or chest.

When the ball is coming toward you, go forward to meet it. If you wait for the ball to reach you, a defender might step in front and intercept it. After you make contact with the ball, relax your body and give way slightly. Some coaches tell their players to "treat the ball like an egg" (you handle an egg with care, so it doesn't break). Of course, you should keep your eyes on the ball at all times.

Drills

- A good way to practice ball control is to stand with a partner 10 yards apart. The player with the ball tosses it to his or her partner, who controls it with the inside of the foot, outside of the foot, thigh, or chest. Then add motion: The controlling player runs backward, then forward to meet the ball as it is tossed. Later you can add a defender who starts from behind and tries to intercept the ball. This helps you learn to control a ball under pressure.

JUGGLING

Juggling is a great skill to learn. (Think of a circus juggler keeping oranges or knives in the air—except this time it's a soccer ball, and there's only one.) A player who can juggle feels confident every time a ball comes to him in the air) It's another form of ball control—and it's fun.

When you juggle, your body should be relaxed. Keep your weight low, so that you can shift direction easily. Your foot should be pointed upward and toward your body. Bring the ball close to your body on every touch. The most commonly used parts of your body are the instep (top of the foot), thigh, and head.

When you are learning to juggle, don't be afraid to allow the ball to hit the ground. When it bounces, gather it with your foot and keep juggling. Resist the temptation to use your hands.

Drills

- Contests are a great way to learn juggling. Count the number of consecutive or total juggles each person does. You can start with a toss. As you get more experienced, start the juggle by flicking the ball up off the ground with your foot.

- Next, learn to juggle in twos, threes, or more. A fun game is called "Zelmo" (named for the nickname of one of its inventors in the 1970s). Juggle one or two times, then pass the ball in the air to another member of the circle. A player who cannot control the ball, or lets it hit the ground, gets a "Z." The next time, he or she gets an "E." The player who spells "Zelmo" first has to sit out. Keep going until only one juggler is left.

SHIELDING

This skill is often overlooked, but it is crucial. "Shielding" is the ability to keep your body between your opponent and the ball, so that you do not lose possession. Shielding is done when the ball is not moving, or moving very slowly. To shield well, you should keep your weight low; lean over the ball so that you can't be knocked off balance by an opponent. You can use your arms to help shield if they are hanging naturally at your side; you cannot raise them to fend off an opponent.

"Shielding" drill

Drills

- A good game for practicing shielding involves playing in small squares called "grids." Everyone has a ball except for two players. Those two try to kick away as many balls as possible. When your ball is kicked out of the grid, you must leave. In another version of the same game, the players without the ball try to win the ball (called a "tackle," but not the football kind!), keeping it under control. If you lose the ball, you must take the place of the person without it.

PASSING

Passing is one of the most important parts of soccer. It is the best way to get a ball from one player to another. There are many different ways of passing—on the ground (for accuracy); in the air (for dis-

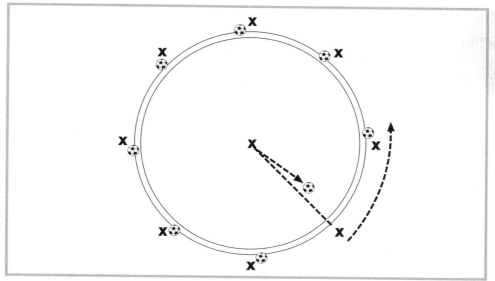

Passing Circle Drill

tance); with the inside of the foot (for power); with the outside of the foot (to curve the pass away from an opponent).

But no matter what type of pass you are making, certain skills remain the same. The body should face wherever you want the pass to go. Approach the ball with a normal running stride. Your leg should swing rhythmically from the knee (not the hip). Your ankle should be locked. Your nonkicking foot should be planted firmly next to the ball, for balance and aim. Be sure to follow through. Your body's weight should be low, with the knee over the ball—except for a long, lofted pass, in which case you should lean back for power and distance. Your pass should be neither too hard nor too soft for a team-mate to handle. Finally, be sure to pass to your teammate's foot, not to open space.

Drills

- To begin practicing passing, find a partner and begin hitting the ball back and forth. Soon you can add a defender, who tries to steal the ball. As you get better, practice with your weak foot.

Add competitive elements: See how many passes you can both make in 30 seconds.

- With more players, put one person in the middle of a circle. Everyone on the outside of the circle has a ball. The player in the middle must receive a pass from each player in a clockwise direction, and pass it back. Repeat, until everyone has had a chance to be the receiver in the middle of the circle.
- Next, have five to six players stand 15 to 20 yards apart from each other. Put one person in the middle ("no man's land"). The aim is to pass the ball to the teammates on the other side without interception. If the ball is intercepted, the player making the pass replaces the one in "no man's land." This teaches long ball passing with accuracy.
- You can also play keepaway, with two teams. Five completed passes by one team equals one goal.

HEADING

Heading is an important technique of soccer. It is done both defensively (to clear the ball away) and offensively (to pass to a teammate or shoot). However, no one should practice it too much. If done properly, heading will not give you a headache. Still, there is no reason to overdo it.

To head properly, watch the ball as it approaches. Keep your eyes open and your mouth closed. "Attack"

the ball to get more power; don't just stand there and let it hit you. Arch your body backward from your waist; swing the top half of your body forward (not just your head), using neck muscles to "throw" the forehead at the ball.

Drills

- To practice heading, find a partner. Stand five yards apart, and toss the ball toward each other's head. Then add a third player. The header should try to redirect the ball to that person.
- You can also add another player, who stands (without jumping) in front of the header. The idea is to get the person heading to jump for the ball, and make contact before it comes down.

SHOOTING

This is probably the most fun part of soccer. After all, the idea is to score more goals than the other team. But shooting is not simply blasting the ball as hard as you can. You need accuracy as well as power. The best shooters in the world shoot low and at the corners, because that's the hardest place for goalies to make saves. (Here's a secret: Goalkeepers hate to dive.)

When shooting, use the instep whenever possible, for power and accuracy. Keep your head down so that you can watch your foot connect with the ball. Also, lean a little bit over the ball. Make sure to follow through—you can even add a little hop-step after your shot—and also follow up your shot, in case you get a rebound off the goalie or the post.

Drills

- To practice shooting, stand in line facing a player whose back is to the goal. Pass the ball back to that player; he or she will pass it back to you. After you get the return pass, take a shot. Practicing with a moving ball prepares you for playing a real game.
- The person who is passing to you can also stand behind you, and roll the ball to you. You can take one or two touches, then shoot.
- You can practice shooting in groups of four. Two of you play one-on-one in a 20-yard area. You try to score on the other two, who stand at opposite ends with their feet spread apart, acting like "goals." After 45 to 60 seconds, switch "goals" and players.
- If you have portable goals, move them in close (30 yards apart). You can play this shooting game in three groups of four to five each. The idea is to shoot quickly and often; the first goal wins. The losing team sits; the team that was sitting out takes their place.

THROW-INS

Throw-ins look easy, but they take practice, and there are several things to keep in mind when making a legal throw-in. You are allowed to take a running start, but when you actually make your throw both feet must be on the ground. The ball must come from behind your head, and it should not spin (both hands should contribute equally to the throw). You also should follow through, to get distance on your throw. Your feet should be spread, and your knees slightly bent. Power comes from strong arm action, with a firm swing of the body from the waist.

Drills

- You can practice throw-ins with a partner. Start close together, then work for distance. Add motion, so that the player throwing in is running forward while the partner who is receiving the throw is running backward.
- You can also play a soccer game with a special twist: The ball can be advanced only by a legal throw-in. Everyone throws the ball to teammates. Players receiving the ball control it with their foot, then pick it up and throw the ball themselves. The only way to score is by taking a legal throw-in past the goalkeeper into the net.

DEFENSE AND TACKLING

So far, we have talked only about offensive techniques, but defense is half the game of soccer. To play good defense, you first must have good positioning. This means keeping your body between the ball and the goal. Your body should be half-turned to the ball; do not face it square-on. Again, your weight should be low. When you make a tackle, watch the ball—not your opponent. Crouch forward slightly; plant your nontackling foot firmly on the ground next to the ball, and try to strike the ball in the middle. Keep your body firm; don't lunge at the ball.

Drills

- You can practice tackling in pairs, close together, to get your timing and technique down. As you gain confidence, you can try to dribble past the other player, who tries to tackle the ball cleanly. Begin 10 to 15 yards apart. When the whistle blows, move toward each other.

PRACTICE GAMES

I n addition to drills, there are lots of good games that help develop
skills. For example:

FREEZE TAG

Each player with a ball dribbles in a grid, or the center circle. One
player does not have a soccer ball; he or she is "it." A player who gets
tagged by "it" must stop and hold the ball over his or her head, with
their feet spread apart. A teammate can "unfreeze" a player by dribbling the ball through his or her legs.

COACH TAG

Players dribble in a grid or the center circle, trying to avoid being
tagged and frozen by the coach. This is a good way to practice fakes,
changes of speed, and protecting the ball.

Freeze Tag

HUNGRY HIPPOS

All the players except two start out on one end line. Everyone has a soccer ball except the two "hippos," who stand 10 to 15 yards away. The goal for everyone else is to dribble past the hippos to a "goal line" 20 to 25 yards away, while they try to kick the balls away. A player whose ball gets kicked away becomes another hippo. Continue until only one dribbler remains.

OBSTACLE COURSE

Anyone can set up a creative obstacle course that involves knocking passes off benches turned on their sides, dribbling around cones, shooting a ball, and sprinting after it, etc. The object is to beat your own best time—don't worry about anyone else's.

3-VS.-3 OR 4-VS.-4 ROUND ROBIN TOURNAMENTS

Play one-goal games, with winners staying on.

3-VS.-1

Three players try to pass the ball around, and knock over a cone defended by one player. The defender must not be close enough to touch the cone. Count the number of goals scored in five minutes; then switch, and make another person the defender.

4-GOAL GAME

Play this on a small field. Each team has two small goals to attack, and two to defend. This encourages quick changes of direction and plenty of shooting.

MANY GOAL GAME

Set up several small goals at random around the field. Divide into two teams. Either team can score on any goal, from any direction.

However, for a goal to count, the ball must be passed through and controlled on the other side by a teammate.

3-TOUCH GAME

Each player is allowed only three touches; five completed passes by one team equals a goal. This is good for controlling passes, passing, and thinking about what will happen next.

SOCCER GOLF

Set up a "course" that involves long and short passes, traps, water hazards, etc. Your imagination is the limit.

SMALL-SIDED SOCCER

Full-field games with 11 players on each team are not the only way to play soccer. Small-sided games (also called "short-sided" soccer) are considered great training for young players. This is the way European and South American youngsters have always learned the game. Many youth leagues across the country now play small-sided soccer. It's every bit as real as 11-against-11 soccer. U.S. coaches, players, and parents are now realizing something the rest of the world has known for years: Soccer is soccer, no matter how many (or few) players you have on the field.

Small-sided soccer refers to three vs. three through six vs. six soccer. Games are played on small fields, generally half the size of regulation or less. Small goals can be used, or cones placed five yards apart (with cones, the ball must go in on the ground to count). There are no goalkeepers. "Positions" are less exact than in 11-vs.-11 soccer; every player is expected to play both offense and defense. Games should last no more than 40 minutes. There are no offsides; all fouls are taken as indirect kicks.

Players like small-sided soccer for many reasons. They get more "touches" on the ball. They also get more chances to make quick decisions (whether to pass, dribble, or shoot; who to pass to, etc.).

Soccer is as much about thinking as it is about running or scoring. (Of course, in small-sided soccer, there are many more chances to score, so that's fun too!)

In small-sided soccer, everyone has to work hard, so it's great for conditioning. There's less emphasis on winning; more on just playing.

Coaches like it too, because it teaches the game well. Small-sided soccer is really what big-sided soccer is all about. A game of 11-vs.-11 is not *really* 11 against 11. It's a lot of little duels: You try to beat one player, you pass off, your teammate loses the ball, she gets it back from a defender, then she and you work a two vs. one and score. Small-sided soccer is just another form of full-field soccer.

Coaches also like it because players learn to call their own fouls and to shoot low. And small-sided soccer can be played anywhere; you don't need a huge field, or even goalposts.

LAWS OF THE GAME

In soccer, rules are not rules—they're called "laws." There are only 17 of them, and all except one are pretty simple. (The complicated one is called "offside." We'll get to that later.)

Here are the Laws of the Game.

LAW 1: THE FIELD OF PLAY

A regulation soccer field should be between 100 to 130 yards long, and between 50 to 100 yards wide. There also must be a midfield line,

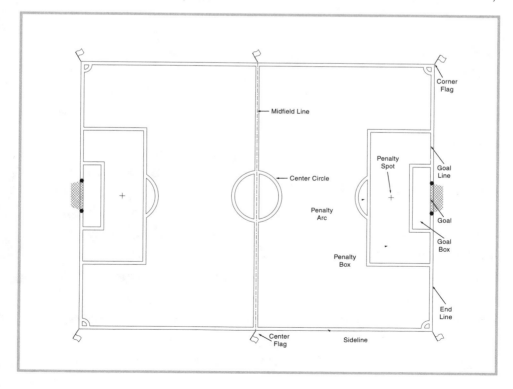

a goal area extending six yards from each goalpost (the ball is placed inside this area for a goal kick), a penalty area extending 18 yards from each goalpost (a goalkeeper can use his or her hands here), and a corner area (for taking corner kicks). The rule also says that each goal should be eight feet high and eight yards wide.

Of course, many youth teams play small-sided soccer. In those cases the field will be much shorter—sometimes less than half regulation size. The important thing is not how big the field is, but that you have some place to play.

LAW 2: THE BALL

This rule says a ball should be made of leather "or other approved materials." It also specifies the proper size and weight. A regulation soccer ball is called a size five; younger players use smaller soccer balls, sizes four or three.

LAW 3: NUMBER OF PLAYERS

A regulation soccer game consists of two teams of 11 players each, one of whom must be a goalkeeper. In international soccer, the number of substitutes is limited to two or three, but in many youth leagues there is "unlimited substitution" (players can leave and enter a game as needed).

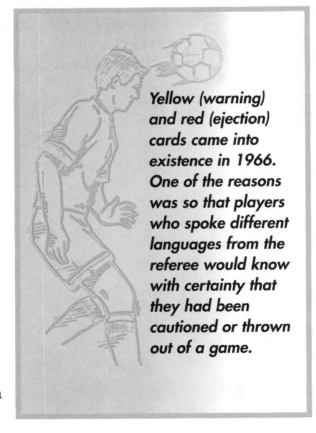

Yellow (warning) and red (ejection) cards came into existence in 1966. One of the reasons was so that players who spoke different languages from the referee would know with certainty that they had been cautioned or thrown out of a game.

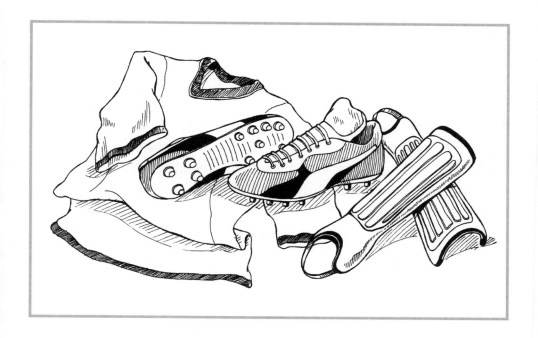

LAW 4: PLAYERS' EQUIPMENT

This law says that players must wear jerseys, shorts, socks, shoes, and shin guards. The goalkeeper must wear colors that are different from teammates and opponents. The reason is that a goalie is the only player allowed to use his or her hands, so the referee must be able to see who exactly is handling a soccer ball in a crowd.

LAWS 5 AND 6: REFEREES

Yes, the refs are covered by the laws. These laws say that every game must have a referee, and explains his or her duties (enforcing the rules, keeping time, cautioning players, preventing injuries). In professional soccer there is one head referee on the field. He or she has two assistants (they used to be called "linesmen"), whose job is to run the sidelines and signal out-of-bounds and other infractions. However, in many youth and high school games there are two equal referees on the field.

LAW 7: DURATION OF THE GAME

A regulation match consists of two 45-minute halves. Younger teams may play shorter halves. If the score is tied after regulation, leagues and tournaments may choose to play overtime. This can be up to two 15-minute periods, or "sudden death" (also called "golden goal"). If the score is still tied after overtime, some tournaments may be decided by penalty kicks. Each team takes five kicks, with five different shooters; if the score is still tied, there are "sudden death" penalty kicks. The MLS in the United States is experimenting with a shootout after overtime. Players start 35 yards away from the goal, and have five seconds to shoot and score.

LAW 8: THE START OF PLAY

This rule simply says that at the start of each half, and after any goal, play begins with one team kicking the ball, which is placed at midfield.

LAW 9: BALL IN AND OUT OF PLAY

A ball is out of bounds when the entire ball crosses the goal line, end line, or sideline, either on the ground or in the air. Even if it comes back into play, it is considered out of bounds, and the other team gets the ball.

LAW 10: METHOD OF SCORING

A shot counts as a goal only if the entire ball has crossed the goal line. The referee must be absolutely certain he or she has seen this happen. This is sometimes difficult when a ball hits the inside of the post or the underside of the crossbar and rebounds on the line.

LAW 11: OFFSIDE

Here it is: the most difficult rule in soccer. The idea of offside is to prevent "goal hanging" (one player waiting in front of the opponent's net for a pass). Basically, a player is offside if he or she is in the attacking half of the field, and does not have at least two opponents (the goalkeeper can count as one) between him or herself and the ball. However, a player can be in an offside position and not be called offside, provided that that player is not part of the play, and the opponents are not defending the player, or distracted by him or her. Also, offside can be called only on a pass or a shot; it cannot be called while a player is dribbling. This allows a player in an offside position to scramble back onside.

LAWS 12, 13, AND 14:
FOULS AND MISCONDUCT; FREE KICKS; PENALTY KICKS

There are nine fouls that result in a direct free kick: Kicking or attempting to kick an opponent; tripping an opponent; jumping at an opponent; charging an opponent violently; charging an opponent from behind; hitting, attempting to hit, or spitting at an opponent; holding an opponent; pushing an opponent; and hitting, catching, or

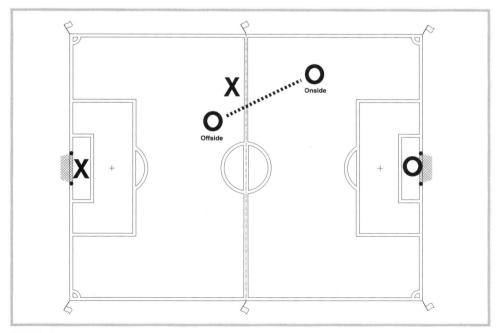

Offside Law

carrying the ball with one or two hands (unless you are a goalkeeper and are in the penalty area).

The penalty for any of these nine fouls is a direct free kick. The opposing team puts the ball down, plays it, and can score a goal immediately without anyone else touching the ball. If one of those nine fouls takes place in the penalty area, then the direct free kick becomes a penalty kick. The ball is placed 12 yards away from the goal, and any one player on the team that was fouled is allowed to take a penalty kick. The goalkeeper is allowed to move sideways before the ball is kicked, but cannot move forward.

There are other fouls that result in an indirect free kick: Dangerous play (for example, trying to kick the ball when the player or an opponent is on the ground); obstruction (not allowing an opponent to play the ball); and unsportsmanlike conduct (this includes swearing, even at yourself; yelling at an opponent or the referee, and wasting time). Goalkeepers can be called for indirect free kick fouls, too, if they take more than four steps before releasing the ball, or hold on to it for more than six seconds.

Though today's soccer balls actually weigh an ounce more than earlier ones, they seem lighter, because with plastic coating they do not retain water.

The penalty for any of those fouls is an indirect free kick. The opposing team puts the ball down, plays it, but cannot score a goal unless a second person—anyone on either team—touches the ball first. If one of those fouls takes place in the penalty area, it is still an indirect free kick; nothing changes.

Players can also be cautioned by the referee. A player who receives a yellow card is

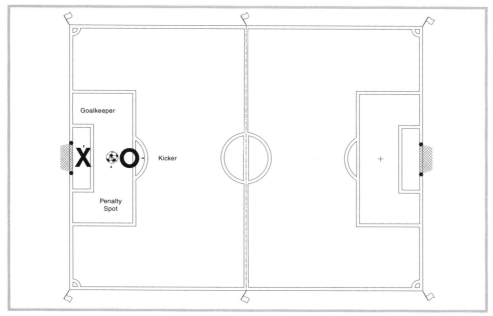

Penalty Kick

considered "warned"; anyone who receives two yellow cards in one game, or a red card for a particularly violent foul, must leave the match. They cannot return, and they cannot be replaced, so their team must play a "man down."

LAW 15: THROW-IN

When the entire ball goes out of bounds on the sideline, the other team puts it back in play with a throw. A player throwing the ball in must face the field of play; both feet must remain on the ground, and the throw must come from behind the head, without spin.

LAW 16: GOAL KICK

When a team takes a shot that does not enter the goal, but goes over the goal line and out of bounds, the other team receives a goal kick. The ball may be placed anywhere in the goal area, and any player can put it back in play by kicking it out of the goal area.

LAW 17: CORNER KICK

When the defending team kicks the ball out of bounds over its own goal line, the other team gets a corner kick. The ball is placed anywhere in the small quarter-circle near the corner flag, and is kicked into play. A goal may be scored directly off a corner kick, although this is extremely difficult. When it happens, it usually comes off a header.

LAW 18: ADVANTAGE

There are only 17 laws. However, soccer referees follow another, unwritten rule, Law 18: The Advantage. If one team commits a foul, but the other team would suffer if that foul is called, the referee may yell "Play on!" and let play continue. In other words, if you were racing to goal on a breakaway and got tripped 30 yards away, but kept both your balance and the ball and cruised in alone on an empty goal, the referee would not call the foul; he or she would let you play on. Blowing the whistle would give the other team time to set up a defensive wall and get the goalkeeper back in place, so you and your team would actually be at a disadvantage.

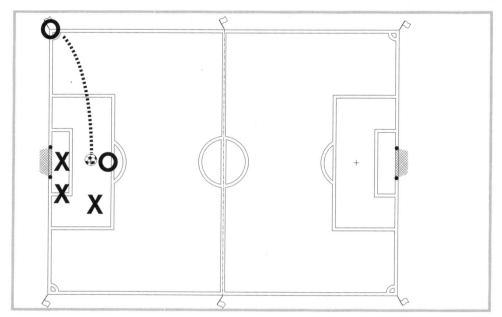

"O"'s corner kick is intended for the teammate at the top of the penalty box.

The term "offside" comes from an English expression "off their side." Because the English word for team is "side," players who were not where the rest of the team was—in other words, hanging near the goal mouth when the rest of the play was near midfield—were "off their side."

Part IV
Overtime

PROFESSIONAL SOCCER LEAGUES

If you think that the MLS (Major League Soccer) is America's only pro soccer league, think again!

MLS

This is the United States's premier professional soccer league. Play began in April 1996, with 10 teams. The New England Revolution, Columbus Crew, New York/New Jersey MetroStars, Tampa Bay Mutiny, and (Washington) D.C. United were in the Eastern Division, with the Dallas Burn, Colorado Rapids, Kansas City Wizards, Los Angeles Galaxy, and San Jose Clash in the Western Division. Miami and Chicago received the first two expansion franchises. Plans are to increase the number of teams to 16 by 2003. Teams play 32 regular season matches, followed by a playoff series culminating in the MLS Cup championship in October. Each club is allowed five international players.

USISL

This is the United Systems of Independent Soccer Leagues. From its start in 1986 as a five-team regional indoor league, USISL has grown to more than 130 teams in five leagues across the country. The leagues are the A-League (highest level), D3 Pro League, Premier Development League, W-League (women), and I-League (indoor). Plans are under way for a Y-League for youth players. The USISL is the official development system for MLS.

NPSL

This is the National Professional Soccer League, founded in 1984. It is an indoor league, whose season runs from October to April.

ORGANIZATIONS

L etters are as much a part of soccer as goals and cleats. Here are a few of the important ones you should know.

FIFA This stands for Federation Internationale de Football Association. That's French for the International Football (Soccer) Association. FIFA was formed in 1904 to bring together all the different soccer playing countries of the world. Today 198 different nations belong to FIFA— more than have joined the United Nations. Today FIFA is in charge of 150 million registered soccer players, including 10 million women. FIFA governs every part of the game. It sets the rules, organizes competitions such as the World Cups for men, women, and youth players, and establishes standards for referees. FIFA is headquartered in Zurich, Switzerland.

CONCACAF This stands for the Confederation of North, Central America, and Caribbean Association Football. It is the regional part of FIFA that the United States and Canada belong to, along with 36 other countries stretching to Guyana in the south. (Other parts of the world have their own regional confederations.) CONCACAF organizes the qualifying tournament for the World Cup for countries in this part of the world, along with tournaments for women and youth players. The Gold Cup is CONCACAF's major event.

USSF This stands for the U.S. Soccer Federation, the national organization for soccer in the United States. USSF is part of FIFA. It oversees all soccer in the United States. The goals of USSF are to make soccer the number one sport in this country and to win the World Cup by 2010.

USSF joined FIFA in 1913. Today 3 million youth players are registered with USSF, along with 300,000 senior players. USSF organizes seven national teams: the full men's team; men's Under-23 (Olympics); Under-20; Under-17; and five-a-side (Futsal); and the women's national and Under-20 teams.

The USSF also registers referees (74,000) and coaches (72,000). Its headquarters are in Chicago.

USYSA This stands for the United States Youth Soccer Association. It is part of the USSF. Its job is to organize all youth (ages 5 to 19) soccer activities in the United States, including national championships for Under 20, 19, 18, 17, and 16 boys' and girls' groups, as well as Olympic Development programs. USYSA also coordinates the activities of 250,000 coaches and thousands of referees. It suggests policies, such as small-sided soccer for players under the age of 10. Underneath USYSA are 55 different state associations (one for each state, and two for New York, Pennsylvania, Ohio, Texas, and California). These state associations are divided into four regions: I (East); II (Midwest); III (South); and IV (West). The USYSA is based in Richardson, Texas.

ODP This stands for Olympic Development Program. It is the path most players take to the Olympic and national teams. Players first try out for a state ODP team. From there they are selected to one of four regional teams, and then for the national team.

AYSO This stands for American Youth Soccer Organization. It is part of USYSA, but runs its own programs. The slogan of AYSO is "Everyone Plays." Most of its programs are recreational, with teams balanced each year to ensure fair competition. It was founded in 1964. Today there are more than 560,000 AYSO players, with more than 260,000 adults serving as coaches, referees, and administrators. AYSO is based in Hawthorne, California.

SAY This stands for Soccer Association for Youth. It was founded in 1967, and is a recreational program. There are now more than 6,500 teams nationally, in seven age groups for boys and girls. Every SAY player must play at least half of each game. SAY is based in Cincinnati.

AWARDS

There are several important awards given each year in American soccer. They are:

FIFA AWARDS

FIFA, the international governing body of soccer, gives out several awards each year at a star-studded banquet.

FIFA began naming a World Player of the Year in 1991. More than 100 national team coaches participate in the voting, making it the most prestigious soccer award in the world. Previous winners include Lothar Matthäus, Marco Van Basten, Roberto Baggio, Romario, George Weah, and Ronaldo.

FIFA also presents a Fair Play Prize to a player who displays excellent sportsmanship, Fair Play diplomas and trophies to various countries (the United States women's team won the Fair Play trophy in 1996 for their performance at the Olympic Games), and awards to two national teams: the best national Team of the Year and the Most Improved Team of the Year. Those two awards are determined by a complex ranking system.

U.S. SOCCER MALE AND FEMALE ATHLETES OF THE YEAR

Each year, the USSF selects its top male and female players of the year. The awards are based on performances on the field, sportsmanship on and off the field, and contributions made toward popularizing soccer in the United States.

The awards are presented as part of the U.S. Olympic Committee's SportsMan and SportsWoman of the Year awards. The soccer nominees are eligible for Olympic Committee awards.

The first men's recipient, in 1984, was Rick Davis. He was one of the first American players to be recognized internationally. He was followed by Perry Van der Beck (1985), Paul Caligiuri (1986), Brent Goulet (1987), Peter Vermes (1988), Mike Windischmann (1989), Tab Ramos (1990), Hugo Perez (1991), Marcelo Balboa (1992), Thomas Dooley (1993), Marcelo Balboa (1994), Alexi Lalas (1995), and Eric Wynalda (1996).

The women's award began in 1985, with Sharon Remer. Other recipients include April Heinrichs (1986), Carin Jennings (1987), Joy Biefeld (1988), April Heinrichs again (1989), Michelle Akers-Stahl (1990 and 1991), Carin Jennings Gabarra (1992), Kristine Lilly (1993), and Mia Hamm (1994, 1995, and 1996).

HERMANN TROPHY

The Hermann Trophy is presented annually to the top NCAA Division I male and female players of the year. Winners are selected in a vote by college coaches and soccer sportswriters.

The trophy is named for Robert Hermann, one of the founders of the NASL. Of the 30 male winners since the first (Dov Markus of Long Island University in 1967), 20 are current or former U.S. national team members. The list of winners includes Glenn Myernick of Hartwick College (currently a pro coach in the MLS), Tony Meola of the University of Virginia, Alexi Lalas of Rutgers University, Brad Friedel of the University of California at Los Angeles, and Claudio Reyna of the University of Virginia. Al Trost and Mike Seerey, both of St. Louis University, Ken Snow of Indiana University, and Mike Fisher of the University of Virginia are the only two-time winners. The schools that have produced the most winners, with five each, are St. Louis University and Indiana University.

The women's Hermann Trophy was first awarded in 1988, to Michelle Akers of the University of Central Florida. Since then, only Mia Hamm of the University of North Carolina has won it twice. The University of North Carolina is also the only school to be represented more than once. Tar Heel athletes have won the women's award an impressive five times.

MISSOURI ATHLETIC CLUB AWARD

The Missouri Athletic Club Sports Foundation Collegiate Soccer Player of the Year is awarded annually to one male and one female player, by the Missouri Athletic Club of St. Louis. Winners must be U.S. citizens (by birth or naturalization). College coaches vote on the award. Every winner has been a U.S. national teams program player.

John Kerr, Jr. of Duke University won the first men's award in 1986. There have been only two repeat winners: Ken Snow of Indiana University and Claudio Reyna of the University of Virginia. The University of Virginia leads the men's list with five recipients.

The women's award was first presented in 1991, to Kristine Lilly of the University of North Carolina. Her teammate Mia Hamm is the only two-time winner. The UNC Tar Heels also lead the list with four recipients.

INDEX